Nail Your Public Speech

Essential Steps for New and Aspiring Speakers

Soulaima Gourani

Nail Your Public Speech

First published Soulaima Gourani – 2024

Copyright © 2025 Soulaima Gourani

All rights reserved. No part of this publication may be copied or reproduced in any form, by any means, electronic or otherwise, without prior consent from the copyright owner and publisher of this book.

First edition

Table of Contents

Introduction 4
1, 2, 3 get Started! 13
Your Message and Audience: Targeting with Precision 20
Unpaid Gigs 25
Setting the Right Price 27
Your speakers Bio 31
Equipment and Preparation 37
Contracts 42
Your presentation 44
Final Thoughts for the Pro Speaker 48
You Can Do This! 50
How to Become an Expert and Thought Leader 61
Speaking Secrets from the World's Best 79
Look for inspiration in the history books 82
Your Next Step 101
The Final Word 113

Introduction

Picture this: an empty stage, framed by heavy red curtains, and me, just a kid in the 3rd grade, talking to an imaginary audience. I stood there, in my parents' hotel, pouring my heart out to rows of empty chairs, rehearsing speeches only I could hear. Back then, I wasn't performing for anyone but myself, discovering the thrill of stepping up, speaking out, and pretending that every seat was filled.

Fast forward to today. If you're thinking about becoming a speaker, you might find yourself in that same place imagining, practicing, and wondering if you can stand in front of real people and bring your voice to life. Becoming a speaker isn't just about perfecting words; it's about owning that stage, filling the space, and knowing that every story you share has the power to connect, change, to inspire.

So, whether you're starting on an "empty stage" of your own or already speaking to packed rooms, remember that first step. Every great speaker began somewhere - often with just a whisper of a dream and a lot of courage. Now, it's your turn. The world is waiting for your voice, and it's time to bring that imaginary audience to life.

When the spotlight is on you, what's your message? What do you feel passionate about sharing with the world?

I've always had a lot to say, though, as a teenager, not everyone was thrilled to hear it. Back then, I was often encouraged to dial it down. Ironically, it's my voice and opinions that have fueled a global career, taking me to over 50 countries and putting me on over 2.000 stages alongside Fortune 500 companies and at prestigious events worldwide.

Today, I'm fortunate to call this my career: speaking, advising, writing, and serving on corporate boards. This path has taken me to inspiring places, introduced me to remarkable people, and given me a unique sense of freedom. And while it sounds incredible, it didn't happen overnight. My journey began in 2001. My first paid speaking engagement came when I was still employed full-time. I'd take a day off to step onto a stage and then return to work the next day. What started as a side gig quickly became a calling, eventually leading me to share stages with icons like the late Sir Ken Robinson, Malala Yousafzai, Arnold Schwarzenegger, HRH Crown Princess (now Queen) Mary, and many more.

I even became a TED Fellow Mentor and built an online community in Scandinavia to help others find their voices.

People often ask how to become a sought-after speaker, commanding high fees, sometimes $12,000 to $30,000 an hour, and having more requests than they can accept. I understand that dream. But to make people want to pay you, you must stand out in ways that go beyond polished delivery. You need a spark, something that makes audiences lean in and remember you long after you leave the stage.

For those of you who have something at heart, a dream, a mission, a message, yet lack formal training or experience, know that speaking success is built over time, with dedication. Today, I have two agents, one in Europe and another in the U.S., but this didn't come quickly or easily. Building a speaking career takes careful, consistent work. Public speaking is often cited as one of the most common fears people face.

The true reward comes from the work itself. There's no richer experience than the opportunity to teach, inspire, and elevate others. As I grow older, the joy of sharing what I know and watching others succeed only grows stronger. Communication is a powerful key - one that opens doors to influence, opportunities, and change. Why learn how to do public speaking? Whether you're speaking to colleagues, pitching a product, or aiming to impress an audience, the goal is to create a bond. Never shy away from taking the stage.

I dropped out in 7th grade, and I don't have a great deal of traditional education. Don't get me wrong, I've received awards and attended executive programs at Ivy League schools. But deep down, I still feel like the girl who grew up in foster care, the one who faced poverty and homelessness. English is my third language, and my words are plain. By most standards, I'd have every reason not to jump on stage. But the truth is, I'm relatable to so many because my life has been a journey through trauma, challenges, and endless hurdles.

The most powerful way to stand out as a speaker is simply to be authentic. Too often, presentations are stripped of personality and delivered like machines to a room full of real people. Corporate culture pushes us to stuff slides with jargon and buzzwords, reading them off as if that's "effective communication." But let's be honest, those phrases we see on so many slides? They sound hollow like we're hiding behind words instead of reaching out.

Real communication happens when there's a genuine connection between the speaker and the audience when we share common values or experiences. Presentations are one of the rare chances for this connection, where we're all in the same room, sharing a moment. Embrace that chance to be real and relatable, and your impact will be lasting.

Here's a question to kickstart your speaking journey: What topic could you talk about for 45 minutes straight, with zero preparation? Think about something you're so passionate about or experienced in that you could dive in without notes. Now, consider if there's an audience willing to pay for that knowledge or insight.

This is often a great starting point for choosing a speaking topic. The topics that come naturally to you, the ones you're excited to share, are often those that resonate most powerfully with an audience. And remember, when people see your passion and expertise, they're more likely to connect with your message. So, what's *your* 45-minute, no-prep topic?

One of the world's best storytellers is Marshall Ganz from Harvard. Years ago, I was fortunate enough to study public speaking under his guidance, and the lessons have stayed with me ever since!

Years ago, when I was awarded Denmark's Best Speaker, I was shocked, moved, and deeply honored. For an underdog like me to be recognized in that way? It proved to me, and hopefully to others, that being real can be more powerful than any polished performance.

My best advice: you must be brave enough to hold an opinion, say it out loud, and be okay with others not agreeing with you.

Practice Makes Perfect

Everyone starts with just one follower, one listener, or one person in the audience. If you're not afraid of the possibility that no one might see, listen, or show up, then you truly have nothing to fear and everything to gain. Remember, everyone begins with just one!

Very few people are born with a natural talent for communication, especially in public speaking. Mastery is built on practice, not luck. Aim to spend at least 20 minutes each day sharpening your speaking skills - even better, dedicate a couple of hours when you can. My number one piece of advice? Get out there and speak. Just like any skill, public speaking skills can quickly grow rusty without consistent use. Becoming truly skilled takes time and intention. Even now, I'm continually working to improve. I take voice lessons, engage in language training, and set new learning goals each year. I also work with top mentors who challenge me to grow. Public speaking is like a sport: it requires the same kind of discipline, training, and commitment.

I remember when my fifth-grade English teacher pointed out that no one could tell if I was saying "beer" or "bear." Speaking English always made me a little nervous, and in 2005, after barely speaking it for over 15 years, I actually hired a private tutor to relearn it. I sat there close to tears as she tried to get me to pronounce words like "condolences" and "curiosity." Language certainly didn't come easily to me.

Today, I host a self-organized online show every Saturday for the World Economic Forum, where I interview world leaders, politicians, thought leaders, and business executives, and yes, it's all in English. Learning English again, putting in the work, and finally moving past (most of) my nerves has been liberating. It has expanded my "playground" in ways I could never have imagined.

Think of public speaking as a muscle. You don't walk into a gym and lift 100 pounds on day one. It takes repetition, patience, and incremental progress. Each time you step onto a stage or in front of a group, you're building strength and confidence, making each future performance a bit smoother.

Experience is built through hard work and learning from mistakes. The best speakers know how to handle the unexpected, whether it's an audience member stepping out, a phone going off, or even an impromptu moment of connection, like a hug from an audience member. Remember, you're there to create an unforgettable experience - not to hold yourself above the audience. Keeping your content fresh is essential to holding attention. Change up your approach regularly, and incorporate new visuals, stories, or questions that keep people engaged. With today's shortened attention spans, these elements make a huge difference in keeping your message dynamic and your audience engaged.

Lastly, don't be afraid to improvise and adapt your talk based on the room's energy. Skilled speakers use the atmosphere in the room to enhance their delivery. Stay open and remember that no two talks should be the same - each audience deserves a performance that feels tailored and alive. Public speaking is a journey, and every step you take brings you closer to becoming a powerful, memorable communicator. For underdogs like us - stepping into public speaking, and mental preparation is KEY. Your audience doesn't want to be re-traumatized by your story, they want to learn from it.

"Teach from the scar, not the wound," as the saying goes. Step onto the stage only when you've had time to reflect, understand, and make meaning from what you've been through. At that point, you're ready to teach, motivate, and inspire others with true impact.

Nothing is more powerful than someone who has been the "first" to face a challenge and now shows others the path forward. Whether it's losing weight, biking alone across Africa, building a business from scratch, overcoming cancer, raising five kids as a single parent, or bouncing back from bankruptcy, your experience can empower others to take on their challenges. When you speak from a place of wisdom and resilience, your story becomes a source of strength for everyone listening.

Take yourself seriously, but not too seriously. Make room for self-forgiveness when you inevitably do something awkward or clumsy. Do you have an embarrassing speaking story? Ever lost your place mid-sentence or blanked out in front of an audience? Trust me, I've been there.

At that time, I confidently started with, "It's so great to be here in Næstved!" only to realize I was actually in the city of Nakskov. Or the time I sat patiently, watching as the previous speaker went way over time, eating into my slot. I finally had enough and nearly marched up to take the microphone from him...only to realize I was in the wrong room altogether!

Embrace these moments - they make you real, relatable and remind you (and your audience) that even the best speakers make mistakes.

When people ask me, *"Who's the best speaker you've ever met?"* or *"Who left the biggest impact on you?"* It's not an easy question to answer. I've been to hundreds of conferences, spoken at over 1,000 events, and for 12–13 years, my life revolved around speaking 3–4 days a week, sometimes in multiple locations on the same day.

But despite all that, one of the most unforgettable speakers I've ever seen was someone you'd never expect. It was many years ago at the MAD Conference in Copenhagen, organized by my friend René Redzepi, a Danish chef and co-owner of the three-Michelin star restaurant Noma. I wasn't speaking, I was simply part of the audience. On stage was a renowned French chef who barely spoke English. He had a translator sitting discreetly under the table beside him because the table was filled with ingredients, props, and tools for his talk.

Throughout his presentation, he'd pause mid-sentence, look down, and ask his translator, *"How do you pronounce this?"* or *"What's the word for that?"* There was no pretense, no polished performance, just raw, authentic communication. And it was one of the most moving, brave talks I've ever witnessed.

That experience taught me something invaluable: if I ever lose my way on stage, forget what I was supposed to say, or struggle with pronunciation, I simply pause and ask for help, even from the audience. There's power in vulnerability. Authenticity connects far more deeply than perfection ever could.

The Truth About Great Speakers: A polished bio doesn't guarantee a powerful performance - especially when it's wrapped in a bad attitude.

Here's what truly matters when choosing a speaker:

Growth Mindset > Past Titles Skills can be learned. Attitude? That's non-negotiable.

Adaptability > Experience The best speakers don't just deliver, they evolve.

Work Ethic > Fancy Degrees Passion fuels impact more than any diploma ever could.

Failure > Perfection Navigating choppy waters builds resilience. Smooth seas rarely create remarkable stories.

Team Player > Difficult Genius Speaking is a team sport - agent, client, audience. A collaborative spirit beats a lone genius every time. Your speaking career isn't rooted in what's been done before. It's built on what's possible.

In this book, I'll share some of the best keys I've discovered along my journey.

In the end, anyone can be a great speaker. It's not about flawless delivery; it's about genuine intention. That's what truly matters.

1, 2, 3 get Started!

The best way to improve your public speaking is to start doing it. Real progress comes from experience, from standing in front of an audience again and again. No matter how much you prepare, true confidence comes from practice.

Another powerful way to grow is by observing skilled speakers. Watch TED Talks, keynotes, or recorded speeches. Every speaker has unique quirks and strengths. They won't all be perfect, but each one can teach you something, sparking ideas for your approach. Push yourself to improve by creating small speaking challenges. Start a weekly group where you and colleagues give short, informal talks on anything - from a recent article to an emerging trend. This exercise will surprise you with how much skill it can build over time.

Take a few minutes daily to write freely about whatever's on your mind. This isn't just journaling; it's a way to build fluency in expressing ideas. Over time, this habit will help you feel more confident and natural when speaking, making your message even stronger.

Here's a step-by-step mindset-building process designed to help you grow into confident, compelling speakers:

1. Embrace Your Story

- **Mindset Shift**: Recognize that your unique background is your superpower, not a limitation. What you've been

through and what you've learned gives you a distinctive voice that can resonate deeply with others.
- **Action**: Write down key moments in your life that shaped who you are. These don't have to be flashy; they're the experiences that make you, you. Reflect on how these stories can add richness and relatability to your message.

2. Build the Resilience Muscle

- **Mindset Shift**: Resilience isn't just bouncing back - it's thriving under pressure. Underdogs often already have a well-developed resilience muscle. Channel it.
- **Action**: Practice speaking in low-stakes environments to get comfortable with discomfort. Speak in front of friends, record yourself, or even talk in the mirror. Each time you put yourself out there, it's like adding weight to that muscle.

3. Reframe Your Nerves as Fuel

- **Mindset Shift**: Rather than viewing nerves as a threat, see them as the energy you can channel into enthusiasm. Even seasoned speakers get nervous; they just learn to use that energy.
- **Action**: Before you speak, take a moment to acknowledge the nerves. Label them as "energy" instead of "fear," and visualize channeling that energy to fuel your talk.

When you're feeling nervous before a speech, important meeting, or exam, many experts suggest taking deep breaths and trying to "calm down." But an intriguing experiment by Harvard professor Alison Wood Brooks shows that the key isn't to suppress your nerves by telling yourself to "stay calm." Instead, try saying, "I'm excited, nervous, and ready."

This subtle shift can make a big difference. Those stress hormones they can enhance your performance, helping you focus and deliver with more energy than if you were entirely calm. Embrace the nerves, they might just be your secret weapon!

Speak more slowly than you think you need to! Adrenaline has a way of speeding you up more than you realize.

4. Focus on Connection, Not Perfection

- **Mindset Shift**: Great speakers aren't flawless; they're relatable. Shift from trying to impress to trying to connect. This makes speaking feel less like a performance and more like an exchange.
- **Action**: Instead of rehearsing to be "perfect," focus on making eye contact, reacting to the audience's body language, and being present now. Practicing vulnerability - such as admitting when you're nervous - often draws the audience in.

5. Adopt a Growth Mindset

- **Mindset Shift**: Public speaking isn't a fixed talent but a skill you build with effort. Every talk is a learning opportunity.
- **Action**: After each speaking experience, jot down three things you did well and one area for improvement. Celebrate the progress, no matter how small, and commit to refining your craft over time.

6. Visualize Success and Feel the Impact

- **Mindset Shift**: Imagine the impact of your message rather than fearing judgment. Picture someone in the audience being inspired or gaining insight because of you.
- **Action**: Before speaking, take a few moments to visualize someone benefitting from what you have to say. This shifts the focus from self-consciousness to the value you're bringing.

Speaking of impact. How do you currently document the impact of your talks and presentations, in other words, how do you measure the effect of your talk?

Many speaking agents emphasize that speakers who track their impact build credibility and stand out in the market. Some effective methods include gathering audience feedback, tracking engagement metrics (like Q&A participation or follow-up requests), or conducting pre- and post-event surveys to measure changes in understanding or motivation.

Testimonials and social media shout-outs are great proof that you're making an impact and establishing your authority as a speaker. And don't forget to snap some photos! (Just ask the audience first, nobody likes surprise paparazzi). It's an easy way to show that, yes, you really are getting booked and people show up to hear you speak!

These steps can turn fear into fuel, build resilience, and channel a sense of purpose, key mental shifts that can empower any underdog to own the stage. Next, if you want to be a speaker, folks must know you're one! Stick 'Public Speaker' in your

LinkedIn bio, slap it on your socials, and don't forget the business card. Boom, now people know they can book you!

While you're waiting for the bookings to roll in, don't just sit back, build your presence and create opportunities!

Here's what you can do to get out there and let people know you're ready to speak:

1. **Set Up Your Digital Home Base**: Build a simple homepage that tells your story, shows off some clips, and makes it easy for people to get in touch. Think of it as your virtual handshake.
2. **Get Loud on TikTok and YouTube**: Share bite-sized insights, stories, or advice. Let people see you in action and connect with your energy, platforms like these are goldmines for visibility.
3. **Shoot for a TEDx Talk**: TEDx events are happening all over the place. Apply for a local one and get ready to hit the stage. A TEDx talk can be a powerful door opener.
4. **Host a Free Webinar**: Take the lead and gather a small crowd around a topic you love. The goal isn't to make money here but to make connections and show what you bring to the table.
5. **Network Like a Pro**: Hit-up events (even virtual ones!) where potential clients hang out. Strike up conversations and let them know you're the next speaker they've been looking for.
6. **Team Up with Other Speakers**: Reach out to other speakers or podcast hosts and offer to jump in as a guest. It's a perfect way to expand your reach.

7. **Write and Share Your Ideas**: Start a blog, and post on LinkedIn. When you share what you know, people start seeing you as the expert.
8. **Collect Social Proof**: Any past speaking gigs? Grab a testimonial! Even a couple of lines can make a difference when people are considering hiring you.
9. **Launch a Newsletter**: Build a list of people interested in your ideas and share tips, stories, and updates with them. Staying in touch keeps you top of mind.

Remember, visibility is key! Don't wait to be discovered - take every chance to share your voice, show your value, and grow your following. Your future clients are out there; make it easy for them to find you!

Also, consider giving participants something tangible to take home, something that extends the impact of your presentation. Many clients print one of my workbooks and place it on each participant's chair, allowing them to dive deeper into the content even after the event. This can be a powerful tool for keeping your message alive beyond the presentation.

You might also consider sharing a printed copy of your slides or a summary handout. Just ensure the client is on board with covering the printing costs! If the presentation is virtual, providing e-codes or a downloadable PDF of key takeaways allows participants to stay engaged, no matter the format.

Offering materials that reinforce your message can significantly increase your influence and credibility. Many successful speakers create "signature" workbooks or guides that align with their core topics. I personally have five different workbooks, each tailored to the audience and topic at hand. Agents also recommend including actionable steps, reflection questions, or checklists to help participants immediately apply what they've learned.

People do love practical tools, advice, tips, tricks, and "models" that people can use. What models, life advice or methods do you share that others find valuable and memorable? What insights do you bring that people truly remember you for?

Your Message and Audience: Targeting with Precision

When planning your speaking career, ask yourself: Who do you envision in those seats? Who truly benefits from your message, and are they the same people willing to pay or book you for speaking engagements?

1. How are you identifying your ideal audience? Is it individuals, private clients, or corporate groups? Tailoring your message to the right audience is key, and often there's a difference between who benefits from your insights and who has the budget to bring you on board.
2. What's your plan to fill the room? Consider the best way to reach those who need your expertise most. Are there specific industries, organizations, or demographic groups that align with your message? Think about targeting quality over quantity, the goal is a room full of engaged listeners who connect with your message, not just filling seats for the sake of numbers.
3. What's the cost of reaching your target audience? Marketing can be costly, especially if you're focusing on a specific group. Map out your marketing strategy, and consider if online advertising, industry events, or even partnerships might be most effective.
4. Have you minimized and refined your target audience? Narrowing your focus can increase your impact. Rather

than appealing to a broad group, define your niche. Who stands to gain the most from your insights? Are there specific sectors or job roles that naturally align with your expertise?

By defining your ideal audience with precision, you maximize your impact and appeal, making it easier for clients and organizers to see you as the perfect fit. Remember, an audience that's carefully selected, engaged, and primed to benefit from your message will always have a greater impact than simply reaching for a wide net.

It's crucial to have something worthwhile to say, and to express it in a way that grabs people's attention and leaves a memorable impression. Aim to make such an impact that people feel compelled to recommend you to others. Regardless of the setting, your topic should feel essential, something audiences feel they *must* hear.

If you ever wonder whether others are searching for the words you use in your talks, try typing those words into Google Trends to see how popular they are. Many years ago, when I started talking about "strategic networking," it wasn't a known term, or when I introduced "Life Design", it's never easy to invent new words or concepts, but once they catch on, you might end up being recognized as their "inventor." Either way, it's a great tool!

Choose subjects you're deeply passionate about, topics that connect with your past, resonate with your audience, and provide enough value that they, or their organization, are willing to invest in learning from you!

- **Have a Mission:** People with authentic passion are far more engaging and credible.
- **Show why *you* are the ideal person to speak on this topic:** Don't hesitate to draw from your personal experiences, your unique story, and what makes your perspective valuable.
- **Market Yourself with Intention:** Be selective with your audience, platforms, and how often you promote yourself. Consistency and clarity build recognition.
- **Deliver a Clear Message:** Use straightforward language and structure your points simply so they're easy to remember. Short stories and vivid imagery can also help make your ideas stick.
- **Be Yourself:** Authenticity draws people in and builds trust. Embrace your unique voice and style.
- **Adapt to Your Audience:** Notice audience reactions and adjust your tone, examples, or pacing to keep them engaged in real-time.
- **Get Regular Feedback:** Keep tabs on how people react to your message so you can tweak and improve. Post clips online and see what comments roll in or ask for feedback after each talk. It might sting a bit sometimes, but honest feedback is where the real growth happens.

Mastering the Art of Feedback

- **Stay Positive (Yes, really!)** Let's be honest - most of us thrive on a little encouragement. But we live in a world that loves pointing out flaws. Sure, take the critiques

seriously, but don't forget to high-five yourself for the wins, too!
- **Be Specific (No Mystery Feedback)** The clearer the feedback, the easier it is to use. Ask for specifics! "Work on this" is fine, but "Here's what to try next time" is where the magic happens.
- **Keep It Real (and Doable)** Feedback is only helpful if it's something you can act on. Look for advice you can use without a total overhaul.
- **Check Their Motives** Before you dive into the feedback, consider the source. Are they looking out for you, or maybe (just maybe) hoping to feel a bit better about themselves? Feedback with good intentions always lands better.
- **Listen First, Defend Later** Hear them out before jumping in with your side. What are they saying? Keep an open mind - there might be some gold in there.
- **Ignore What Doesn't Click (Within Reason)** Not every piece of feedback will feel useful, and that's okay. But if you're hearing the same thing from multiple people, it might be worth a second look.
- **Ask for What You Need** Sometimes we need help in specific areas, but people can't read minds. Don't be shy - ask for feedback that'll make a difference for you.

Feedback doesn't have to be a drag. With a little humor and some self-awareness, you'll be a feedback pro in no time!

We often talk about recording our presentations to analyze how we deliver our message. But here's what many forget: it's not actually about you, it's about your audience. Try filming them while you speak, so you can later observe their reactions to what you say and how you say it. You'll gain so much more insight this way!

How to Connect - fast

Research shows that people judge leaders first on warmth (trustworthiness) rather than competence. This is vital because it aligns with the idea that influence starts with connection, not technical expertise. People often respect competence, but they engage and follow warmth.

When people trust a leader, they're more likely to embrace the message and adopt the organization's values. Competence without warmth, on the other hand, can lead to compliance rather than commitment. Nonverbal cues like nodding, a genuine smile, and open gestures help convey warmth, showing people you're approachable and attentive. These signals can be more powerful than trying to project authority or expertise.

Leaders who exude both strength and warmth are often seen as "happy warriors." They bring calm and confidence, making it easier for people to trust and follow them, even in challenging times.

Unpaid Gigs

Requests for free talks pop up all the time, often from groups with genuine reasons. And while I get the need, and sometimes wish I could say yes to everyone, free talks don't pay the bills. Sure, unpaid gigs can bring fulfillment, but ultimately, you'll want to focus on paid opportunities.

Many speakers start with unpaid gigs to build confidence and visibility. If you're in a city, get creative: hop on the subway, talk to small groups in parks, or even strike up conversations at local events. It's a fun way to practice and get known.

However, remember that once you start giving your work away for free, it can be hard to shift to paid engagements later, unless you make a remarkable shift that boosts your value.

Only consider free gigs when:

- You need the practice: These gigs help you get rid of your stage anxiety, and fine-tune your message, delivery, and presence.
- You're passionate about the cause: If it truly resonates, you may find greater reward in the impact.
- It's a strategic audience: Speaking to the right group can open doors for future paid opportunities.

Turn Lemons into Lemonade; if they can't pay your fee, ask for something in return. Turn the experience into a win-win:

- Need quality photos? Ask if they have a photographer who can take professional shots of you in action.
- Want visibility? See if they'll feature you on their blog or social media, linking back to your site.
- Building your network? Ask for introductions to key contacts they may know who could book you in the future.

The point is to creatively leverage these free talks to build your platform. When people invest in your expertise, whether financially or with valuable exposure, they're more likely to appreciate what you bring. Free talks can be part of the journey, but your voice has value, so don't hesitate to ask for what you're worth in one way or another!

What steps can you take today to ensure that, in a month or a year, you'll be where you want to be in your writing and speaking career?

Setting the Right Price

Pricing your speaking engagements isn't just about a number, it's about capturing the value, experience, and effort you bring to each talk.

When I started speaking in 2000-2001, I charged around 7,000 DKK per talk (about USD 1,000), which soon grew to 12,000-15,000 DKK (USD 1,700-2,200). Today, my fees are well over $20,000. Your pricing should evolve with your demand, expertise, and the sacrifices you make. Speaking isn't only about the time on stage; it's about the countless hours spent on the road, the separation from family, and the reality of sometimes staying in less-than-glamorous hotels, dining alone, and navigating flight delays and long drives. Life on the road, while rewarding, can also be isolating and challenging.

Set your rate to honor the unique value you provide. Think about:

- Your expertise: Price your knowledge and skill set at a level that reflects your experience, preparation, and insights. You're not just "giving a talk" - you're delivering expertise.
- Invest in yourself: You've likely invested time and money in courses, books, and experiences that add to your knowledge. Your rate should reflect that continuous growth.

- Opportunity cost: Every engagement requires you to be away from other potential projects, family time, or rest. Your price should account for what you're sacrificing to be there.

Remember, your fee isn't just a transaction, it's a statement of the value you bring. With each step up in your career, adjust your pricing confidently to match your growth, your influence, and the impact you know you'll have on every audience. Pricing your talks is a delicate balance. Set your fee too high, and you risk fewer bookings; set it too low, and clients may undervalue your expertise. The key is to find that sweet spot where your rate reflects the value you bring while remaining accessible. Aim to adjust and increase your fees gradually each year as your experience, demand, and impact grow. Consistent growth in your pricing signals confidence in your value and helps establish you as a professional worth the investment.

Some might wonder if hiring a professional speaker (you) is worth the investment. Let's break it down, inspired by Kyle Crocco is the Content Marketing Coordinator at BigSpeak Speakers Bureau:

1. **Audience Investment** A conference isn't just a venue and catering. Consider the real cost: the time and productivity your audience dedicates. With just 200 attendees making $60,000 annually, that's around $48,000 in daily salaries alone - plus another $800,000 in lost productivity. So, having a speaker who truly resonates isn't a "nice-to-have"; it's essential to justify this audience investment.

2. **Boosting Registration and Buzz** A recognizable name can make ticket sales soar. Big-name speakers not only add credibility but bring social media buzz, word-of-mouth promotion, and, often, increase ticket sales. My bureau (*BigSpeak) once had a client struggling with ticket sales until we added major speakers. The event went from undersold to a sell-out. In other words, investing in the right speaker can often pay for itself.
3. **Building Credibility for Future Events** Booking a high-impact speaker doesn't just elevate this year's conference; it establishes your event as a go-to. Attendees remember the experience, which can enhance your event's reputation long-term and encourage higher attendance in the future.
4. **Maximizing Audience Engagement** Professional speakers bring expertise, energy, and relevance. Unlike "free" speakers, professionals don't just talk - they engage, inspire, and leave lasting impacts, increasing the likelihood of productivity and morale boosts post-event. Studies show that quality speakers deliver an ROI, often surpassing their cost multiple times over in terms of increased engagement, satisfaction, and even long-term productivity.
5. **Long-Term Value** Surveys reveal that 92% of event planners were satisfied with their speaker investment, with nearly 87% reporting ROI between 1:1 to 5x the speaker's cost. Attendees feel respected and valued with a quality speaker, and that positivity can ripple through teams for weeks after.

So, when "you" invest in a professional speaker, you're not just covering an "extra" expense; you're giving your audience a meaningful experience that drives value, engagement, and impact - both now and into the future.

I hope this information is helpful next time you're negotiating your fee.

Your speakers Bio

Create a speakers bio, it is a concise, downloadable profile that includes your talk topics, titles, key references, and recommendations. This bio acts as a quick introduction for emcees, event organizers, and audiences, capturing the essence of who you are as a speaker. Make it available on your homepage, so emcees can easily download it and use it to give you a warm, well-informed welcome. This "blurb" should be a soundbite-worthy summary that conveys your expertise, personality, and the impact you bring to the stage, making it effortless for others to present you with confidence.

Here is an example of a speaker bio. What I love about it is the effort she makes to include the pronunciation of her name (as someone named Soulaima, I can relate!). She also highlights some of her key innovations and clearly outlines what people can expect to take away from her talk. See image on the next page.

Dr. Thaïs
(ty-ees)

Doctor of Common Sense

As a Christian speaker, Dr. Thais speaks on learning the common sense approach to life's situations, knowing who you are as an individual, and how you can feel more confident by making small improvements and better decisions in your life.

Dr. Thais believes in encouraging and empowering you to aspire to be better, on your own personal level, while sharing the fundamentals of becoming the successful person you were meant to be.

She uses small and simple ways to get you to become a more improved person. Some of the topics she discusses are:

1. Getting Your Faith Feet Wet;
2. Changing the Atmosphere; and
3. Steps to Revival.

Dr. Thais is a blessed wife and mother of two, who loves to find something to smile about and encourage others. Her daughter Laila, has been a professional DJ since she was seven-years-old and she is currently writing a book. Her son Zachary, has been producing music since he was eight-years-old. Dr. Thais is also an inventor.

Bookings/Contact Info:
p: 850.325.0220
w: DrThais.com
e: DrThaisSpeaks@gmail.com
fb: Facebook.com/DrThais

If you'd like a simpler version, let the following serve as your inspiration:

Dr. Alex Rivers - Leading Expert in Green Energy Inspiring Speaker on Sustainable Innovation

Bio for Emcees Dr. Alex Rivers is a renowned green energy expert and keynote speaker, celebrated for making complex sustainability challenges accessible, engaging, and actionable. With over 20 years in the renewable energy field, including consulting with major global organizations and contributing to policy frameworks, Dr. Rivers combines deep expertise with an infectious passion for sustainable innovation.

Dr. Rivers has spoken at [mention prominent conferences, e.g., "the United Nations Climate Change Conference, TEDx, and Clean Energy Summit"] and is regularly featured in publications like *National Geographic*, *Forbes*, and *Scientific American*. Known for a style that's both enlightening and entertaining, Dr. Rivers brings a grounded, relatable approach to the latest advances in green tech and sustainable practices, inspiring audiences to think differently about the future of our planet.

When Dr. Rivers speaks, audiences walk away not only more informed but motivated to take real, impactful actions in their personal and professional lives.

Key Topics:

- **Future of Green Energy**: A look into cutting-edge technologies transforming the energy sector, including breakthroughs in solar, wind, and battery storage. This talk challenges audiences to imagine a future powered entirely by renewables.

- **Sustainable Innovation in Business**: Practical strategies for organizations looking to embrace sustainability without sacrificing profitability. Dr. Rivers shares case studies from companies leading the way in green transformation.
- **Climate Resilience and Adaptation**: A powerful session on preparing for a sustainable future in the face of climate change. Dr. Rivers offers insights into climate adaptation strategies that businesses and communities can implement today.

What Others Are Saying "Dr. Rivers captivates the audience with a rare blend of expertise and authenticity. His talk on the future of green energy didn't just inform - it inspired a full room of executives to take action." - Sarah Lee, CEO, GreenWorks Consulting

"Alex Rivers makes sustainability exciting and accessible. His session on climate resilience was one of the best I've ever attended - practical, engaging, and full of real-world insights." - David Chen, Director, Global Energy Forum.

You get the point, right!

Your Speaker Photos: Make Them Count

Let's talk speaker photos. These pictures should be professional and engaging, because nothing says "boring" like a stiff headshot! A great speaker photo should reflect your personality and approach, giving audiences a sense of who you are before you even step on stage. Update your photo every 2-3 years and avoid using anything too outdated. Nothing is more awkward than seeing a headshot of someone in a program, only to find that, in person, they look 20 years older. Keep it current and authentic.

It's also smart to include a photo of yourself in action, ideally in front of an audience. This shows that you're experienced, comfortable, and dynamic on stage. If you haven't had a chance to speak to a big crowd yet, don't worry! Gather some friends, set up a little "audience," and snap some shots of you in full speaker mode. A great speaker photo should look natural, inspiring, and true to you.

I have a fun routine where I snap a photo of the audience from the stage and ask everyone to wave. I tell them it's for my mom, who still thinks I should get a 'real job.' It always gets a good laugh.

Also, remember your speaker bio and press photos don't have to be boring!

Equipment and Preparation

Every venue presents its unique setup - some are fully equipped with state-of-the-art AV gear, while others may have the essentials or even less. As a speaker, adaptability is crucial. Establish a clear set of AV requirements with the organizers well in advance, but also be prepared to adjust on the fly.

To ensure a smooth experience:

- **Specify Your Essentials**: Confirm with organizers that the necessary equipment - like microphones, lighting, and monitors - will be available. I always provide a detailed list of my needs to minimize surprises.
- **Coordinate with the AV Team**: Reach out directly to the AV team before the event. Share your specific hardware setup, presentation format, and any video files in advance. This helps them understand your requirements and anticipate any technical challenges.
- **Test Your Visuals and Sound**: If your presentation involves multimedia, check for rights and permissions, then rigorously test everything beforehand to avoid disruptions. Decide if you'll permit attendees to film or photograph you and communicate this to the organizers.

Always have a "go-bag" with everything you need to succeed: a clicker for your slides, your microphone if you prefer it, your laptop, and a backup of your presentation on a USB stick (or stored in the cloud). Prepare for the worst-case scenarios - and be ready to present without slides if needed.

This summer, I arrived at a talk, only to find my slides wouldn't load. No problem - I'm comfortable delivering with or without visuals. The key is to avoid becoming a slave to your presentation. Things will go wrong; technology will fail but remember: the audience is there for *you*. Be prepared, adaptable, and confident enough to command the stage on your own. Finally, in the past, I've made the mistake of rushing in and out of engagements, often missing out on speaking to those who booked me or some in the audience. Now, I make it a priority to arrive at least 30 minutes early and to stay afterward for questions and networking. This small adjustment has significantly boosted my connection with the audience and added real value to each event. For international engagements, I ensure I arrive the day before to be well-rested and jetlag-free. Why? Because every talk is an opportunity to build future bookings.

A successful talk should naturally lead to 3-4 new inquiries, and staying afterward gives you a chance to gather feedback, create memorable moments, and connect with potential clients. This time is invaluable - not only for securing follow-up engagements but also for understanding the audience's perspective on your message.

Be Unforgettable

The best speakers don't just deliver a talk, they create an experience that stays with their audience long after the applause ends. How? Through energy, stories, real pictures (like from your childhood, something original - not a stock photo) memorable moments, and an authentic connection.

Even if your topic is serious, a little laughter goes a long way. It doesn't have to be the content itself that's funny, just find ways to help your audience relax and lighten up. A well-timed joke or a lighthearted comment can break the tension and make your message even more impactful. I've found that if I can get a few laughs within the first minute, I've got their attention and engagement right from the start.

Energy as a Catalyst

Your energy on stage is infectious. It's what sets you apart, the invisible force that keeps eyes on you and ears tuned in. Great speakers harness this energy to ignite the room, making their message not only heard but *felt*. Think of your energy as your "silent message" - even before you say a word, your energy already speaks volumes. Walk on stage with purpose, make eye contact, and let your enthusiasm shine. The best speakers maintain this energy, using it to lift the room and keep the audience hooked.

As a speaker, how you spend the moments before going on stage can make all the difference. Avoid distractions like checking your phone or reading emails that might upset you. Instead, rest, breathe deeply, and focus on things that make you happy - watch a quick, uplifting video of puppies if needed. Energize your body language by raising your arms overhead and warming up physically. These small actions set a positive tone, helping you bring your best self to the stage.

Creating Memorable Moments

Memorable speakers craft moments that linger. It might be a powerful story, a surprising fact, or a well-placed joke, but it's always something that breaks the flow just enough to make the audience stop and *feel*.

The key is to make your talk more than information - it's an experience. To make it memorable, ask yourself: what can you give your audience that will change them in some way? That might be inspiration, insight, or even laughter, but it must be real and leave a mark.

Connect with your audience by finding common ground. Have you been to their city, state, or country? Mention it! Maybe you've worked in their industry, or you share a quirky experience. For me, as a Dane, I love how often people tell me they're 'Danish' - and when I dig a little, it turns out their great-great-grandfather was Danish! But hey, it's a connection, and it makes the conversation fun and relatable. Be creative, find those little ties, and let your audience see you as one of them.

I remember speaking to a crowd of 500 women at a telecom company, and it didn't even cross my mind to mention that I'm a mom. Later, I wondered, why I didn't share that part of myself. In a room with 500 women, there were surely other moms in the audience. You see what I mean? Sometimes, connecting on a personal level is as simple as sharing a common experience.

What the Best Speakers Do
The most impactful speakers make their message crystal clear, often through stories that make complex ideas feel personal. They speak with authenticity, conveying a strong sense of

purpose. They also actively engage the room, reading the energy and adapting their approach on the spot. They pause to let key points sink in, they vary their tone, and they watch their audience to see if they're connecting.

Great speakers also know that emotions are what people remember. People may forget facts, but they never forget how you made them *feel*. Craft your message to inspire, challenge, or comfort - and know that every word, pause, and gesture contributes to that emotional connection.

My friend Amy Cuddy, a professor and an expert in body language, delivered one of the most-watched TED Talks out there. I've learned so much from her. Find someone inspiring, stick close, and soak up all you can

Be Intentional with Your Energy, Your Stories, and Your Purpose

If you want to be unforgettable, show up fully, bring your best energy, and make every moment matter.

Great speakers don't have 'off' days - or at least, they don't let it show. I'm not necessarily proud of this, but I spoke on stage the day after my father passed away and the day after losing my sister. No matter the day or circumstance, I can step up and deliver.

Engage with your audience like it's a conversation, give them stories they can connect with, and deliver it all with purpose. When you're intentional about your energy and authenticity, you don't just deliver a talk - you create memories and connections that people will carry with them. That's what makes a speaker truly memorable.

Contracts

Keep contracts straightforward and client-focused, setting clear expectations from the start. Prompt payment is key, so consider a little incentive, some speakers send a small thank-you gift, like chocolates, for on-time payments.

For international clients, platforms like PayPal or Wise simplify transactions and avoid currency hiccups.

And when it comes to travel, try pre-booking arrangements through the client to sidestep upfront expenses. These simple strategies help keep cash flow steady and relationships strong.

- **Terms in Black and White:** Define the event details - date, location, duration, and scope of your talk - so both sides know exactly what to expect.
- **Fee Structure & Payment Terms:** Set your fee, deposit requirements, and payment deadlines. Mention any perks for timely payments and penalties for late ones.
- **Travel & Expenses:** Specify who covers travel and lodging. Whenever possible, arrange for the client to book accommodations to avoid upfront costs.
- **Recording & Usage Rights:** Clearly outline if the event can record, share, or publish your talk online. Specify whether they need your permission to distribute it or use clips for promotional purposes.

- **Cancellation & Force Majeure Policy:** Detail fees for cancellations or rescheduling and what happens in case of unforeseen events like illness, natural disasters, or pandemics. A force majeure clause can protect you financially if circumstances outside your control, such as a health crisis, prevent the event from taking place.

Your presentation

Let's talk briefly about your presentation. It's all about igniting change! Designing a stunning presentation has never been easier. Not long ago, you'd need a designer to make your slides look professional. Now, with tools like Google Slides, Canva, and others, anyone can create eye-catching visuals with ease. One of my favorite presentation experts, Nancy Duarte - an acclaimed author, speaker, and CEO - puts it best in her book Slide:ology.

Most businesses begin with a visionary spark, an idea of how they can make the world a better place. And here's where your presentations come in! Communicating these changes, visions, and strategies is crucial. It's not just about sharing data, it's about inspiring action, building buy-in, and rallying everyone around a common vision.

So, whether it's a high-stakes keynote presentation or a casual presentation in your local soccer club, use that time to persuade, inspire, and set folks on a path. So, take the stage and make your presentations count!

As a speaker, understanding the Misinformation Principle, Gibson's Principle, and the Incentive Filter is crucial, not only for building your credibility but also for ensuring your message resonates authentically and responsibly.

As a speaker, your credibility is everything; it's the bridge between you and your listeners. By grounding your message in solid facts and being aware of the misinformation out there, you not only position yourself as a trustworthy voice but also help cut through the noise that bombards your audience daily.

Audiences today are savvy, and they can spot empty buzzwords and vague claims from a mile away. Presenting well-researched, clear information shows you respect their intelligence, making them more likely to connect with and trust you.

Always have in mind just because someone has a title, or degree doesn't mean they have all the answers. For speakers, it's a reminder that true authority comes from insight, not just credentials. Audiences connect with speakers who offer value, not just titles. Relying solely on credentials can create a barrier between you and your audience, while relatable, well-explained information breaks down that barrier.

You can put up a slide with every award, title, and PhD you've got, but here's the real question: do they trust you? And remember, "For every PhD, there's an equal and opposite PhD." So, let the emcee handle the bio and the applause for all those accolades. From that point on, focus on why you're worth their time. Nothing derails a talk faster than someone dropping "I went to Harvard" six times.

As a speaker, you're often competing against a sea of "experts." By focusing on genuine value, clarity, and humility, you'll build a reputation for insight that resonates far more than credentials alone.

Every piece of advice or information has a motive behind it. For speakers, this is a reminder to stay transparent about what's driving your message. Are you speaking to educate, inspire, or promote a particular agenda? Audiences appreciate speakers who are upfront about their motivations and who keep their message aligned with the value they want to offer.

Audiences today are quick to question motives and bias and with good reason. By clearly articulating your "why" and aligning it with your audience's needs, you reinforce your authenticity and gain their trust.

Also, remember you can't tell your story without touching on parts of others' stories as well. As a speaker, it's important to be mindful of this, to share your experiences while respecting the privacy of others involved. Consider how you frame each story to ensure you're honoring their boundaries, avoiding unnecessary details, and keeping the focus on your journey and insights.

I typically speak for around 7 minutes per slide. Each slide is paired with a complete story, one with its own beginning, middle, and end. This way, if I get interrupted or need to cut things short, the audience still gets a clear message from each slide. The key takeaway should never be left until the very end, only after all slides are shown. How do you structure your slides and manage your timing?

On my slides I share my social media handle, @soulaimagourani. This way the audience can post and share insights during my talks. I also let them know that if their question doesn't get answered on the spot, they can post it on X, and I'll respond there. This approach not only helps the content go viral but also makes the audience feel like they have direct access to me.

Your title?

Ever thought about giving yourself a title beyond 'public speaker,' 'keynoter,' or 'motivational speaker'? Here are ten innovative, upbeat options to make your title truly stand out:

Story Shaper - crafting narratives that captivate and inspire.

Inspiration Architect - building frameworks for motivation and change.

Impact Navigator - guiding audiences to discover their own potential.

Momentum Maker – energizing people to take meaningful action.

Transformation Catalyst - sparking breakthroughs and fresh perspectives.

Vision Alchemist - turning ideas into tangible plans for the future.

Challenge Coach - empowering people to overcome obstacles and grow.

Connection Curator - fostering authentic relationships and engagement.

Resilience Mentor - championing the power of persistence and adaptability.

Possibility Pioneer - exploring new ideas and opening doors to opportunity.

Final Thoughts for the Pro Speaker

- **Be Driven by Purpose:** Have a meaningful message that resonates - this is why clients book you and audiences remember you.
- **Know Your Worth:** Set your fee confidently and stick to it. Respecting your own values reinforces your brand.
- **Stand Out:** People remember those who stand for something unique. Embrace what makes you memorable and lean into it.
- **Celebrate Your Quirks:** Your quirks aren't flaws; they're your signature. Don't dilute what makes you distinct.
- **Build Your A-Team:** A skilled assistant, diligent accountant, and savvy bookkeeper are investments in your success.
- **Learn to Say No:** Protect your energy and time; you don't have to accept every opportunity (note to self, too!).
- **Maintain Your Presence:** Secure your name as a domain, keep your website fresh, and stay active on platforms like X and LinkedIn where clients can connect with you.
- **Invest in PR:** A strong personal brand can take you far. When possible, invest in PR to share your expertise widely.

Mastering the art of speaking means finding your unique edge and never losing sight of it. Stay bold, stay original, and let every word make an impact.

A book, blog, podcast yes/no?

Publishing a book is a powerful tool for landing speaking engagements. E-books are a fantastic option, easy to create and distribute on platforms like Amazon. One of my e-books has sold over 800,000 copies! While I've had the pleasure of writing traditional books with publishers (I've contributed to over 26 so far), self-publishing is easier than ever. So, why wait for a publishing house when you can share your insights with the world right now? A blog and podcast, same point!

Success in the speaking world isn't a solo act. Partner with others who challenge you and help you stay relevant. Sometimes, stepping back is necessary to reimagine your message and refresh your approach.

Stay in tune with your market. Are you still engaging, impactful, and memorable? Regularly gather feedback to understand how your audience perceives you.

You Can Do This!

When people say you're "too much," it's often because they feel they're "too little." So, grab that mic, step up, and let your voice be heard. Remember, each time you stand before an audience, you're receiving a precious gift: their attention. Treat it with respect, empathy, and energy. No audience is too small or unimportant, and a great speaker lifts the room, releases energy, and shows a new path. Your job is to take your listeners on a journey they'll never forget.

See Your Audience as in a positive light

Imagine your audience as vulnerable but hopeful - people who want to be seen and recognized. Ask yourself, "What do they need more of?" Sometimes it's as simple as gratitude. Recognizing your audience's needs opens them up to your message, making it land deeply.

Every time you step on stage, take a moment to pause, look out at the audience, and let it all sink in before you begin speaking. Show them that you genuinely care. If you're feeling a bit nervous, go ahead and admit it, being human builds connection. Embrace the pause, be authentic, and let them see the real you.

Stage nerves? Normal. But here's the thing: "Fear is for the ego." It's the ego that fears looking foolish. Let go of that and focus instead on genuine connection. Your body language says it all. Avoid fidgeting, pacing, or gestures that reveal unease. Speak to the heart. People connect with emotion, not endless data or complex jargon. Often, charisma and a sense of genuine connection make a bigger impact than sheer expertise.

Preparation Before Showtime Matters

Studies show that people perform better when they prepare with "big things" like power poses or stretching than when they're hunched over small screens. Before you step up, stretch, smile, and channel positive energy. Think of yourself as an "energy anchor" for the room, someone who sets the tone. Walk the space, greet a few people, and make eye contact. When you bring good energy, your audience will mirror it.

I sometimes like to step off the stage and move among the audience. If it feels natural to you, try it it's a powerful way to connect and bring energy into the room. Your opening words are everything. Ditch the filler actions like throat-clearing or fumbling with the mic. Imagine a launch countdown: 3, 2, 1 - boom! Your first words should ignite the room. Today's audiences expect speakers to be genuine, and to speak from the heart, not a script. If you want your audience to care, you must care just as deeply.

Natural talent helps, but discipline and practice are what set-top speakers apart. As Carol Dweck's research shows, talent without perseverance can limit long-term success. Embrace the awkward stages of learning, which are just part of the journey to mastery. From Martin Luther King Jr. to President Trump, the world's most impactful speakers hone their craft through relentless practice. Public speaking is your personal growth project, so watch TED talks, study techniques, and imitate styles until you find your unique voice.

Speaking slowly is associated with power. The more powerful you feel and the more powerfully others feel you are. Use pauses effectively.

Public speaking ranks high on the list of human fears, right alongside death. People dread exclusion or judgment. But here's the paradox: vulnerability is what draws others in. Embrace the discomfort, stand tall, and keep pushing forward. The more you do, the more resilient and connected you become. Public speaking isn't just an act; it's a journey into self-discovery. Storytelling is humanity's oldest tradition, and it bonds us in unique ways. For you and your audience, it's part of what makes us human.

Watching recordings of yourself can feel brutal, but it's worth it. Reviewing your performance helps you find areas to improve and highlights your strengths. Each critique builds confidence faster than any other tool. It may be uncomfortable, but it's essential for growth.

Your appearance matters. Feel great. Get some professional photos and attire that aligns with your brand. Think of your look as part of your communication; each detail should enhance, not distract from, your message.

And don't forget your online presence. Make sure it's cohesive and aligns with your message. Whether on X, LinkedIn, or your website, present yourself in a way that builds trust and connection. Make your message relatable and timeless. On stage, credibility is a given when you're prepared and confident. Forget justifying your experience; get straight to the message. Audiences today don't care as much about your credentials - they care about authenticity and impact.

To keep your credibility:

- Maintain open, confident body language.
- Dress to support your message.
- Keep your content engaging and relevant.

Above all, remember that people connect most deeply with your energy, your message, and your authenticity. Stay grounded, believe in what you're saying, and your audience will believe in you, too.

In a Harvard session I was taught something my professor called "Oprah Time," I learned the power of creating intimacy with an audience. As speakers, we all want our audience to feel, *"This person really gets me."* Here are some key takeaways on how to make that happen:

Speak to People, Not History

- *Connection over content*: People aren't looking for historical facts - they want a personal connection. Aim for authenticity so that your audience feels a genuine "I like them" sentiment.

The Power of a Duchenne Smile

- True smiles, known as *Duchenne smiles*, engage muscles around the eyes, not just the mouth. Try a tip: biting a pen between your teeth can mimic a real smile and even boost your mood.
- Beware of *fake smiles*, which only contract around the mouth and don't reach the eyes, audiences pick up on this. However, when facial movement is restricted, such as with Botox, the brain's ability to read others' emotions

can be impacted. For speakers, this reinforces the importance of authentic facial expressions. Being able to smile, frown, and respond expressively can deepen your connection with the audience, making your message more impactful and relatable.

The Strength-Warmth Balance

- Some people project strength naturally, while others project warmth. The ideal is finding natural moments to express both traits authentically. Your hands, gestures, and expressions should align to avoid looking disingenuous.
- Example: In a study, one client learned to talk about his son as part of his keynote which helped him connect with his audience on a personal level, adding warmth to his strong professional demeanor. I always include a picture of my family in my talks, it helps make me more relatable.

The Importance of Chit-Chat and Small Talk

- Research shows that talks with a balance of chit-chat and business are more successful. Small talk isn't trivial, it builds rapport and eases tension. Don't skip the chance to connect on a personal level before diving into content.

Non-Verbal Connection Cues

- *Mirroring*: Subtle mirroring, especially with a slight 4-second delay, shows attention and engagement.
- *Eye Contact*: Maintain steady eye contact but be mindful of cultural differences.
- *Immediacy Cues*: Gestures like leaning forward, nodding, or reaching out convey attentiveness and warmth.

Authentic Body Language

- To detect inauthenticity, watch for "asynchronies" mismatches between what's being said and how it's expressed through body language. The more synchronized your expressions, the more trustworthy you appear.

Active Listening and Engagement

- Listening actively doesn't imply deference; it shows respect and interest. Asking questions and showing curiosity fosters a sense of partnership and mutual respect.
- Always take questions, it's a great way to show you're confident and comfortable with your material. However, avoid ending with the Q&A. Instead, plan a strong closing line after the Q&A to wrap up on a high note. This way, you leave the audience with a memorable finish and give them a reason to applaud *twice*.

When you put yourself out there, not everyone is going to throw you a standing ovation. And honestly, that's where most people get tripped up - the hard truth that not everyone is going to love what you have to say. Welcome to life! Learning to handle a few 'haters' is just part of the deal. Here are some super practical tips for handling bad feedback, negative audiences, and (online) trolls effectively:

1. Stay Calm and Centered

- Negative feedback and difficult audiences can feel personal but try to view criticism objectively. Take a deep breath and remind yourself not to react impulsively.

2. Look for Constructive Insights

- Even in harsh criticism, there may be valuable insights. Ask yourself if there's anything helpful in the feedback that could improve your message, presentation, or approach.

3. Separate Constructive Feedback from Trolling

- Constructive feedback is specific and focused on improvement, whereas trolling is typically vague, unkind, or provocative. Identify and prioritize constructive feedback and avoid engaging with trolls who simply want to provoke.

4. Respond with Professionalism and Empathy

- For audience members who seem disengaged or critical, acknowledge their perspective and show empathy without becoming defensive. For example, "I appreciate your feedback; let's dive deeper to address any concerns."

5. Set Boundaries with Trolls

- If online trolls cross the line, set boundaries. Ignoring trolls is often the best response, as engagement can fuel their behavior. If trolling becomes aggressive or harmful, consider blocking or reporting the user.

6. Keep a Positive Tone in Responses

- For negative comments that aren't outright trolling, keep your response positive and professional. This approach often disarms critics and shows your commitment to constructive discussion.

7. Learn and Let Go

- Use feedback to learn and grow but don't dwell on negativity. Once you've taken what's useful, let the rest go and focus on future improvements.

8. Surround Yourself with Positive Influences

- Seek support and feedback from mentors, peers, and supportive colleagues who understand the demands of public-facing work. Positive influences can help you stay motivated and resilient.

Handling negativity effectively is a skill that will enhance your resilience, professional growth, and confidence in your work.

Finally, how to Stand Out as a Speaker?

Every speaker, no matter how experienced, knows the feeling of doubt, that blurry line between confidence and imposter syndrome. Standing in front of an audience can make even the most prepared person question their worth: *Am I the right person to share this? What if they don't connect?*

We all feel that discomfort, that hint of fraudulence that creeps in, especially when facing a new challenge or a larger audience. Public speaking can be a game-changer for your career. It creates opportunities, reveals your true potential, and allows you to share your story and wisdom in a way that inspires others. You don't have to be the best, the most knowledgeable, or an expert. See myself as a third grader speaking to a first-grade audience, and that's okay. The important thing is to step forward, put yourself out there, and share your message with those who need to hear it.

Fear of mistakes, stress, anxiety, haters, doubt, and imposter syndrome - all of these are normal.

- **Embrace and Understand Stress**: Learn techniques to manage nerves and stay grounded.
- **Master Your Thoughts**: Harness positive thinking and self-belief to support your message.
- **Strengthen Your Voice**: Develop a voice that's clear, powerful, and healthy.
- **Establish Real Connection**: Eye contact and authentic presence are your strongest tools.

The first step to great speaking is clarifying what you want to share with the world. Hone in on the topics you're passionate about, the messages that truly matter to you.

Whether live or online, focus on connecting with the audience that needs your message most. **Why Them, Why Now, Why You?** Identify your "product-market fit" as a speaker, ensuring that your unique perspective resonates with the people who are ready to hear it and those who can and WILL pay for it. How can people find you? Position yourself as the go-to expert in your niche and learn how to make it easy for potential clients or audiences to discover you. Have the courage to stand before an audience and command the room. Speaking is about more than just delivering information - it's about sharing your knowledge with confidence and authenticity.

At Harvard University, I was fortunate to be taught by Professor Bill George, who posed a powerful question: *Why are we afraid to share with people who we really are? Why is it so hard?* He suggested some key reasons:

- **Pressure to conform to external roles:** We often feel compelled to behave according to the roles others expect us to play.
- **Fear of vulnerability:** Opening up can be intimidating, as it risks rejection or judgment. Yet vulnerability is a strength that connects us with others.
- **Concern about openness:** We may worry that sharing too much will make others uncomfortable.

As you look forward in life as a speaker, consider which environments deplete you and which allow you to be your authentic self. Do you want to go through life with armor on, constantly guarding yourself, or do you want to live without it, open and vulnerable?

Identify a group of people, at home or elsewhere, where you can be at your worst and still feel accepted. Make time to connect with them regularly. Ask yourself, *who would I call in the event of a great tragedy or a huge success?* Be sure to spend time with those individuals and consider who truly matters to you. Make it a priority to be present for them, just as you hope they'll be there for you on this journey of yours.

How to Become an Expert and Thought Leader

Through my many conversations with leaders across diverse fields of public speaking, they have all revealed practical strategies, personal anecdotes, and timeless principles that can transform how we communicate and connect with others.

Let me share some of them with you here.

First, are you an expert?

Becoming a recognized expert or thought leader is a journey that requires intentionality, persistence, and strategic action. You must deal with three critical pillars:

- Content creation
- Social proof
- Networking

To establish yourself as an expert, you need to share your knowledge publicly. Content creation is one of the most powerful ways to do this. Writing articles, blogging, giving speeches, or creating videos allows you to scale your ideas and reach your target audience effectively. Consistency is key, your content should regularly reflect your expertise and align with the needs or interests of your audience.

> *"It's a lot easier to sort of slap something up on LinkedIn, but if you make the effort to actually pitch and... really try to understand*

> *the editorial style... of a major publication, it's just so valuable in terms of exposure, in terms of branding, and can really become a calling card for you."*
>
> ***Dorie Clark***

Writing books, particularly those published by a reputable publisher, is a significant step that can greatly enhance your credibility and authority. A book serves as a long-form platform to encapsulate your ideas, showcase your expertise, and establish a cornerstone for your personal brand.

Becoming an Author as Part of Your Public Speaking Strategy

Writing a book can be a powerful strategy for enhancing your public speaking career. As discussed in several conversations with thought leaders, a book serves as more than just a collection of ideas, it's a calling card that establishes authority, opens doors, and amplifies your personal brand. While the journey to becoming an author has its challenges, insights from these discussions provide a roadmap to navigate the process effectively.

A well-crafted book is an enduring asset for any speaker. It allows you to encapsulate your expertise and share it with a broader audience, often acting as a ticket to larger stages and more prestigious opportunities.

Traditional publishing lends credibility and prestige, positioning the book, and you, as a trusted resource in your field.

Self-publishing, like this book, while increasingly popular, provides more flexibility and control, making it a viable alternative for many aspiring authors.

The Challenge of Writing in the Age of AI

One of the emerging challenges in today's publishing world is the influence of AI writing tools. Concerns have been raised about the potential of AI to mimic human voices and replace creative processes. For example, one of my friends, a great author and speaker, shared the unsettling experience of having her book uploaded to an AI database without consent, raising ethical questions about ownership and authenticity in the age of machine-generated content. Despite these challenges, the unique human perspective and storytelling ability remain irreplaceable strengths that distinguish great authors.

It's essential to think strategically about trademarks and dedicate time to figuring out how to protect your ideas and intellectual property (IP). Taking these steps ensures your unique concepts are safeguarded and helps build a solid foundation for your brand's long-term success.

Crafting a Compelling Book Proposal

Pursuing traditional publishing? A strong book proposal is essential. Experts emphasize the importance of showcasing not just your idea but your personal story and measurable impact.

Publishers look for authors with a robust reach and platform, this includes your social media presence, professional networks, and the ability to reach a dedicated audience. As one leader shared with me, the proposal should include a mix of life story, impact metrics, and visibility, demonstrating your capacity to market the book effectively.

I've had the privilege of publishing four books through three different publishers, which has given me firsthand insight into the complexities of the traditional publishing process. To truly understand this journey, I've found it invaluable to connect with experienced authors and, if possible, review their book proposals. A well-crafted proposal provides a clear roadmap of what publishers are looking for: a compelling idea, a strong author platform, and a clear understanding of the book's potential audience and impact.

Even better than observing others' experiences is taking the plunge yourself. Start pitching publishers or literary agents to grasp the nuances of how to land a contract. This process not only helps you refine your ideas and positioning but also gives you direct feedback on what resonates with the publishing industry. It's a hands-on way to learn and improve, whether you're preparing for your first book or refining your approach for future projects. While traditional publishing carries prestige, self-publishing has become a popular choice for many authors. It offers greater creative control, faster timelines, and the ability to tailor your book's messaging without external constraints. Both routes have their merits, and the decision depends on your goals, resources, and target audience.

Writing with Purpose

Above all, writing a book should align with your passion and expertise. Choosing a topic that excites you ensures authenticity and keeps you motivated through the writing process. One author shared a cautionary tale about becoming an accidental expert in a topic they didn't love. This underscores the importance of aligning your book with your long-term vision as a speaker and thought leader. I usually dedicate one full day each week to writing and often use my vacations to focus on it as well. When my kids were younger, this was challenging for my spouse, as I would often immerse myself in writing for 14–16 hours straight. Now, things are different. I have more time and a wealth of resources to draw from, hundreds of transcriptions from interviews I've conducted over the years, which provide invaluable intellectual property and material.

Currently, I'm working on my next three books, all co-written with industry experts. Collaborating with others through speaking, interviewing, and writing has been an incredible learning experience. Each conversation deepens my understanding, and each project enriches my perspective. Writing is no longer just a solitary endeavor for me; it's a dynamic process of discovery and growth.

Beyond books, you can also share your expertise through more immediate channels like posting daily articles on LinkedIn, contributing to blogs, or writing for online communities.

I've been writing for *Forbes* for over five years and regularly contribute to newspapers. These platforms not only amplify your voice but also help you build an audience and reinforce your position as an expert. However, it's crucial to ensure that what you write about is something you're genuinely passionate about. A psychologist once shared a story with me: he began writing articles about road rage as a side interest. Over time, he became known as *the* expert on road rage, even though he wasn't particularly passionate about the topic. This highlights the importance of choosing a subject you love, as your enthusiasm will keep you engaged and authentic in your work.

Social Proof: Build Your Credibility

Social proof is the evidence that others recognize you as an expert. This can come in many forms: media features, endorsements, testimonials, or even being associated with credible institutions or groups. It signals to others that you've been vetted and recognized by a respected organization. The goal is to accumulate indicators of credibility that affirm your expertise to others. This doesn't happen overnight but rather through strategic efforts to align yourself with credible platforms, events, and collaborators.

Networking: Cultivate Relationships

Building relationships is another essential pillar of expertise. Networking involves connecting with peers, mentors, and influencers in your field. However, as Clark pointed out, effective networking isn't just about connecting with people like you (bonding capital); it also requires creating bridges to diverse individuals and groups (bridging capital). These connections not only broaden your perspective but also increase your opportunities to collaborate and be introduced to new audiences. Clark advises taking the initiative to host and curate gatherings, which positions you as a central figure within your network. Whether it's organizing events, moderating panels, or simply facilitating introductions, being a host demonstrates leadership and strengthens your reputation.

I frequently host events, and sometimes I even fundraise or secure sponsorships to scale them up and create larger, more impactful gatherings. Whenever I'm traveling, I make it a point to post on LinkedIn, sharing my plans and asking my network for recommendations on who I should meet. This not only sparks engagement but also helps me connect with the right people. If you're interested in exploring this topic further, I've written a book titled *Networking for Underdogs*, which delves into strategies for building meaningful connections, even when you feel like the odds are stacked against you.

The Path to Becoming an Expert

Becoming an expert isn't, as you can tell, about achieving perfection or knowing everything, it's about positioning yourself as a trusted, reliable voice in your field. By consistently creating valuable content, accumulating social proof, and nurturing a diverse network, you can build a personal brand that resonates with your audience. This journey is one of constant learning and adaptation, but the rewards, credibility, influence, and the ability to impact others, make it worthwhile. Leadership is not an innate quality but a skill that anyone can develop with the right approach.

The Power of Passion and Vocal Expression

One recurring theme in my conversations with motivational speakers is the importance of vocal variation and passion.

They emphasize that being confident and sure of your message helps eliminate self-doubt and allows for authentic delivery.

Varying tone and volume, bellowing, whispering, and everything in between, can engage audiences and convey emotion effectively. Practicing these variations helps speakers become more familiar and confident with their voice.

Confidence, however, requires overcoming self-consciousness. One leader shared that recording themselves or practicing in front of a mirror helped them identify and address weaknesses in their delivery.

The key takeaway: passion and preparation trump nerves every time!

The role of voice coaching in public speaking is often underappreciated. By refining tone, improving projection, and exploring vocal variations, voice coaching can help speakers enhance their presence and clarity.

This process is as much about technical improvement as it is about building confidence in one's voice as a tool for storytelling and engagement. The voice is like a musical instrument, emphasizing the need to "play" it dynamically.

Varying tone, pitch, and pace can transform a flat delivery into an engaging performance. Practicing how to use your voice effectively is as critical as preparing your content, an approach that encourages speakers to explore their range and add depth to their presentation style.

Physical presence also plays a significant role. Posture, particularly on panels, is a subtle but powerful aspect of communication. Good posture not only conveys confidence but also establishes authority and presence, creating a more compelling image for the audience.

Listening to one's own voice or seeking feedback from others is an essential tool for growth. While hearing yourself may feel uncomfortable, it's an opportunity to identify areas for improvement. Feedback helps speakers refine their style, strengthen their delivery, and build confidence.

Energetic Resonance with the Audience

Speakers often underestimate the importance of tuning into their audience's energy. One leader I spoke to described the process of creating "harmonic resonance," where the speaker listens to and aligns with the energy in the room. This two-way connection fosters a more intimate and impactful exchange, ensuring the audience feels seen and valued.

Preparation Beyond the Stage

An intriguing takeaway was the use of practices like Qigong to prepare for presentations.

This technique focuses on grounding and building energy, helping speakers project a vibrant presence and stay centered in high-pressure situations. Such preparation highlights the interplay between physical and emotional readiness in delivering an exceptional performance.

Before stepping on stage, I have a ritual that helps me center myself. I like to take off my shoes, stand firmly, and ground myself with deep breaths. I avoid talking, expending unnecessary energy, or looking at my phone, it's all about conserving focus and staying present. I take a moment to visualize walking onto the stage, imagining the energy I want to bring to the audience. Then, I remind myself: *"I get to do this."* It's a privilege, an honor, and a gift to share my voice and connect with others in such a meaningful way.

Be Present and Conversational

Finally, the importance of being fully present and speaking conversationally comes up repeatedly when I talk to great speakers.

Visualizing the audience and addressing them as though in a one-on-one conversation fosters authenticity and relatability. As one leader explained, *"There's really nothing inviting or compelling about a rote, formal explanation."* Presence transforms a presentation from a one-sided lecture into a shared experience.

Many leaders highlight storytelling as the cornerstone of impactful public speaking. Data and charts often fail to connect emotionally, whereas a compelling story can leave a lasting impression. One speaker once shared with me how they eliminated charts entirely from their presentations to focus on human connection, ensuring their message resonated on a personal level. Stories engage audiences, make ideas memorable, and create a bridge between speaker and listener.

The Power of Storytelling

Storytelling is one of the most powerful tools we must connect, inspire, and drive change. Conversations with thought leaders have revealed the multifaceted impact of storytelling, on individuals, societies, and even decision-making. Here's what I've learned about its profound role and how to harness its potential.

Storymaking vs. Storytelling

One key insight is the distinction between *storytelling* and *storymaking*. Storymaking is a participatory approach that empowers people to see themselves as active players in the narrative. It's not just about sharing a story; it's about giving others agency within it. As one expert pointed out, people don't change their minds because of facts, they change their minds because of the emotional connection a story creates.

A prime example of storymaking is the iconic "Just Do It" campaign, which gave individuals the power to see themselves as capable and motivated.

Scientific studies underscore the power of stories. They enhance memory recall by up to 93% and synchronize brain activity between storyteller and listener, creating a shared experience. Stories aren't just entertaining; they engage our brains on a deeper level, building empathy and fostering understanding. This explains why myths and ancestral tales, "subjective truths", have been integral to human culture, teaching us how to navigate the world and avoid pitfalls.

Effective storytelling often follows a clear structure. One expert I know highlights Kurt Vonnegut's classic narrative arc, which includes exposition, rising action, climax, falling action, and resolution. This structure can be applied to presentations, pitches, or even personal stories. For example:

1. **Exposition**: Introduce the context, "We met and discovered…"
2. **Rising Action**: Highlight the challenge or insight, "We were amazed to realize the following…"

3. **Climax**: Identify the critical turning point, "It will be game-changing if we address X."
4. **Falling Action**: Share the solution, "So we created this to achieve that."
5. **Resolution**: Close with confidence "We're certain this can make an impact."

This structure ensures your message resonates and stays memorable!

Authenticity and Honesty

Honesty is essential in storytelling. As one expert put it, "Always be honest. Even if the truth is a sharp knife." Authentic stories create genuine connections, and being truthful, especially with yourself, builds trust with your audience. In a world where stories are increasingly democratized, ensuring they are authentic and inclusive is vital. Underrepresented voices, particularly women and minorities, must be elevated to create richer, more diverse narratives.

The Purpose and Power of Storytelling

At its core, storytelling conveys complex ideas and emotions, builds empathy, and inspires action. It shapes our understanding of the world and provides meaning to our lives. Stories can change hearts and minds, uniting people around shared goals and values. Whether you're trying to convey a vision, lead a team, or drive social change, storytelling is a tool for creating a better world.

To harness the power of storytelling:

1. **Be intentional**: Frame your message with a clear narrative arc.
2. **Make it participatory**: Empower your audience to see themselves in your story.
3. **Be authentic**: Speak with honesty and inclusivity.
4. **Engage emotionally**: Focus on connection over data.
5. **Practice and refine**: Like any skill, storytelling improves with practice.

Storytelling isn't just about entertaining, it's about transforming perspectives, fostering empathy, and inspiring action. By using these principles, you can harness the power of stories to create meaningful change.

You often hear that your audience doesn't want too much detail on slides - minimalist, simple visuals are often recommended. And while that's true in many cases, it's not a universal rule. Hear me out.

During an educational module in Argentina, I had the privilege of attending a session with Prof. Guido Sandleris, Ph.D. in Economics, Columbia University. His presentation was packed with exciting insights and well-crafted slides. Surprisingly, the slide that resonated most with the students was the one with the most numbers.

Why? Because it matched the audience's expectations and preferences. For some, a data-rich slide is a goldmine of insight; for others, it's overwhelming. The key takeaway here is simple: know your audience.

There's no need to oversimplify or "dumb things down" if your audience values depth and detail. Instead, tailor your content to their needs. For some groups, numbers and details will spark engagement and curiosity. For others, simplicity and high-level insights will resonate more.

It's not about following a one-size-fits-all format, it's about understanding who's in the room and delivering what will resonate most with them.

1. **Find Your Niche:** Focus deeply on a specific topic or audience to deliver tailored, impactful content.
2. **Leverage Feedback:** Engage with your audience before and after talks to refine and strengthen your message.
3. **Develop Unique Content:** Create original insights or research that becomes your signature and sets you apart.

Differentiate yourself by being specific, listening to your audience, and providing lasting value.

How AI is Changing the Way We Speak and Share Ideas

As a speaker, your goal is to connect with your audience, inspire action, and share your ideas in a way that sticks. AI is transforming not only how we work but also how we communicate and deliver messages. In the past, software tools were designed to make people more productive, helping with tasks like creating slides, writing notes, or organizing data for presentations. Now, with the rise of AI, these tools don't just help you *prepare*; they can actually do much of the heavy lifting for you.

AI as Your Speechwriting Partner

Imagine you're preparing for a talk, and you need to organize your ideas or craft a powerful story. AI tools, powered by something called Large Language Models (LLMs), can help you draft speeches, structure your message, and even suggest compelling ways to phrase your ideas. Think of it as having a super-smart assistant who can take your raw thoughts and shape them into a polished presentation.

AI for Personalization

One of the best ways to connect with your audience is by making your message personal and relevant. AI tools can analyze your audience's preferences, interests, or even current trends, helping you tailor your talk to their needs. For example, you could use AI to generate examples or stories that resonate specifically with your listeners, making your presentation more engaging.

Practice with AI

AI can also be your practice partner. Tools now exist that can listen to your speech, analyze your tone, pace, and body language, and provide feedback on how to improve. It's like having a coach who's always available to help you refine your delivery and boost your confidence.

AI in the Future of Speaking

As AI continues to evolve, it's reshaping what it means to be a great speaker. In the future, speakers may rely on AI not just for preparation but even during live presentations, think real-time translations, instant data insights, or interactive Q&A sessions powered by AI.

However, here's the most important thing to remember: AI is a tool, not a replacement for human connection. The magic of speaking lies in your ability to inspire, engage, and relate to your audience, something only *you* can do. AI can enhance your skills, but it's your passion, authenticity, and presence that make you unforgettable.

Becoming a Great Speaker in an AI World

To use AI effectively as a speaker:

1. **Embrace it as a helper, not a crutch.** Use AI to enhance your preparation, but don't let it take away your personal touch.
2. **Focus on storytelling.** AI can help craft stories, but only you can deliver them with heart and authenticity.
3. **Stay ahead of the curve.** Learn about new tools and technologies that can support your speaking journey.
4. **Never lose the human connection.** AI can create words, but it's your energy and presence that make an impact.

AI is changing the game for speakers, but the core of great speaking remains timeless: connecting with your audience, sharing your ideas passionately, and leaving them inspired. Use AI as a tool to help you shine brighter, but remember, the stage is yours.

AI-Powered Outbound Sales: The Next Step for Speakers

As a speaker, getting your message out there isn't just about delivering powerful presentations, it's also about finding the right audiences and booking opportunities. Tools like **11x** and **11 Labs**, with their AI bots Alice and Jordan, are revolutionizing outbound sales and can play a crucial role in promoting your keynotes. AI will pose a significant challenge for many speaking agents and bureaus.

As a practical example like "Alice and Jordan" (ai bots from 11x) can help you identify and engage with potential clients by analyzing data on companies, event organizers, and audiences that align with your expertise.

These AI bots can craft personalized, data-driven outreach messages that speak directly to the needs and interests of your target audience. Imagine reaching hundreds of decision-makers with tailored emails or LinkedIn messages that feel personal and relevant, all without the manual effort.

One of the challenges in outbound campaigns / sales is keeping track of leads and maintaining consistent follow-ups.

AI bots can automate this process, sending timely reminders, follow-up messages, and even sharing your speaking reels or past successes. This ensures no opportunity falls through the cracks while allowing you to focus on other aspects of your career.

Take some time to analyze what's out there and identify what strategies would work best for you. The days of relying solely on a basic Facebook campaign are long gone!

Actionable Takeaways for Speakers

If you're considering using AI for outbound campaigns / PR and sales, here are some tips:

- **Start small:** Test AI tools with a specific campaign or audience to see how they perform.
- **Provide input:** Customize the messaging to reflect your authentic voice and brand.
- **Monitor results:** Use the analytics to tweak your strategy and improve outcomes.
- **Stay involved:** While AI can do the heavy lifting, your personal touch and follow-through are still essential for building trust and relationships.

Speaking Secrets from the World's Best

Managing Nerves and Building Confidence

Nerves are a universal experience, but preparation and small rituals can help manage them. One leader described starting with a "speaker kit" containing water, gum, and a small cloth to calm pre-speech jitters. Over time, through experience and preparation, they became more comfortable and self-assured on stage. Managing nerves is less about eliminating them and more about channeling them into focused energy.

Presence and Authenticity

Perhaps the most universal advice was the importance of being present and authentic. Audiences respond to genuine passion and conviction. One leader noted that a lack of presence, described as "flat" delivery or a rushed, information-dense presentation, creates disconnection. To captivate an audience, speakers must focus outward, on the message and the people they're addressing, rather than inward on self-doubt.

Writing Conversationally for Connection

An important insight is the emphasis on writing conversationally. Whether preparing for public speaking or crafting a message for media engagement, adopting a tone as if speaking to one person, sharing coffee or tea, helps create intimacy and relatability. This approach transforms communication from a monologue into a dialogue, fostering a deeper connection with the audience.

Maximizing Media Impact

Another key point is the ability to harness communication skills for media interactions. Presenting authentically and projecting energy in media appearances are essential for amplifying one's message. This requires not only speaking effectively but also embodying confidence and enthusiasm that resonate with diverse audiences.

Stay Relevant

If you're a motivational speaker, staying ahead of the curve is essential. What topics will be relevant 1, 3, or even 5 years from now? Identify those trends, study them deeply, and position yourself at the forefront. I do this by dedicating time each year to immersive educational programs around the world. For 2–3 weeks annually, I focus entirely on learning and growth, which not only fuels exciting new content for my talks but also allows me to apply what I've learned in my work. This often leads to the development of actionable models and frameworks that benefit others.

Additionally, my weekly podcast is a vital tool for continuous learning. It helps me stay informed, build expertise, and share insights with a growing audience while expanding my network. By consistently investing in education and sharing knowledge, I stay relevant, inspire others, and solidify my role as a thought leader in the ever-evolving world of motivational speaking.

Celebrating Multidimensionality

Finally, a crucial takeaway is the value of embracing and celebrating one's full, multidimensional self. Effective communication isn't just about delivering polished messages;

it's about bringing authenticity and passion to the forefront. This authenticity is what leaves a memorable impression, and fosters trust with an audience. Public speaking is not about perfection but about preparation, connection, and authenticity.

Passionate delivery, emotional connection, and a focus on storytelling can elevate any speech. By managing nerves, seeking feedback, and embracing vocal variation, anyone can transform their ability to inspire and engage.

Whether you're a seasoned speaker or just starting out, these lessons serve as a reminder that public speaking is a skill we can all learn and master with practice and intention!

Look for inspiration in the history books

In ancient times, speaking well could mean life or death. Persuasive speech helped people negotiate peace, win leadership, or defend themselves in court. The Greeks formalized it into "rhetoric," and Cicero later perfected it, calling public speaking a tool to inspire, lead, and protect freedom.

Public speaking is a critical skill for executives, essential for conveying ideas, persuading audiences, and establishing authority. Executives often face challenges such as performance anxiety, audience engagement, and information overload. Preparation, tailored content, and strong vocal and non-verbal techniques are key to delivering impactful messages. As digital platforms grow, adapting to virtual speaking is also vital.

Many executives must manage complex dynamics, such as disagreements among leadership, while maintaining professionalism during presentations. Understanding personalities and risk profiles helps tailor the approach and improve outcomes. Additionally, avoiding information overload is crucial - clear, concise delivery of key points ensures clarity and engagement.

A senior manager I mentored at a multinational corporation struggled to assert her voice in executive meetings dominated by male colleagues. To help her build confidence, I introduced her to voice training and speaking techniques through sessions at our local theater. We focused on assertiveness, presentation skills, and strategic ways to interject effectively. As a result, she found her voice, influenced key company decisions, and today enjoys a thriving career at an even larger organization.

A great presentation can draw inspiration from historic leaders who mastered the art of communication. One of my personal favorites is Winston Churchill. Winston Churchill's Address to the Joint Session of the U.S. Congress in December 1941, just weeks after the attack on Pearl Harbor, is often celebrated as a masterclass in rhetoric and statesmanship. Delivered during a critical moment in World War II, the speech was pivotal in cementing the U.S.-U.K. alliance and rallying support for the war effort.

Key Elements Highlighted by Analysts:

1. **Personal Connection**: Churchill immediately establishes a personal bond by referencing his mother, Jennie Jerome, who was American. By doing so, he reminds the audience of his ties to the United States, making him relatable and emphasizing the shared heritage between the two nations. This disarmed his audience and created an emotional connection that set the tone for collaboration.

    - **Churchill's Words**:
      "I cannot help reflecting that if my father had been American and my mother British, instead of the other way round, I might have gotten here on my own." This touch of humor and humility was met with laughter and applause, showing how effectively he charmed his audience.

2. **Unity and Shared Purpose:** He masterfully framed the war as a shared struggle between the two great democracies of the world. This reinforced the idea that Britain and America were natural allies in the fight against tyranny.
3. **Support for the Cause**: His speech was not only inspirational but also strategic. By presenting Britain's resilience and determination while acknowledging the vital role of U.S. involvement, Churchill ensured a deeper commitment from Congress to support the Allied cause.
4. **Rhetorical Brilliance**: Churchill's ability to blend humor, historical references, and a powerful narrative is unparalleled. He balanced the gravity of the war with moments of levity, such as the quip about how the English language unites the two nations.
5. **Impact and Legacy**: His charm, humor, and eloquence earned him standing ovations and immense goodwill, which bolstered public and political support for the war effort. Ultimately, the speech is credited with strengthening U.S. resolve and cooperation, a key factor in the eventual Allied victory.

Why It Matters for us as public speakers:

Churchill's speech teaches us that personalizing your message, understanding your audience, and connecting through shared values can transform a speech into a powerful call to action. His ability to use wit and emotion to rally a nation shows how even in the darkest times, words can inspire hope and unity, and ultimately change the course of history.

Others to be inspired by:

1. **Abraham Lincoln: The Gettysburg Address (1863)**
   - **Why It's Iconic:** In just 272 words, Lincoln redefined the purpose of the Civil War, honoring those who had sacrificed their lives and reaffirming the principles of democracy and equality.
   - **Key Lesson:** Brevity and precision. A powerful message doesn't require a lot of words - it requires the right ones.

2. **Martin Luther King Jr.: I Have a Dream (1963)**
   - **Why It's Iconic:** King combined vivid imagery, repetition, and a hopeful vision for the future in this speech that became a cornerstone of the Civil Rights Movement.
   - **Key Lesson:** Repetition and rhythm. Anchoring your speech with memorable phrases can leave an indelible mark on your audience.

3. **John F. Kennedy: Inaugural Address (1961)**
   - **Why It's Iconic:** Famous for the line, *"Ask not what your country can do for you - ask what you can do for your country,"* Kennedy's speech inspired a generation to embrace civic responsibility.
   - **Key Lesson:** Inspire action. Use aspirational language to challenge your audience to contribute to a greater cause.

4. **Franklin D. Roosevelt: First Inaugural Address (1933)**

- **Why It's Iconic:** During the Great Depression, Roosevelt's assurance that *"the only thing we have to fear is fear itself"* calmed a nation in crisis.
- **Key Lesson:** Address fear with confidence. Acknowledge challenges but guide your audience toward hope and resilience.

5. **Nelson Mandela: Presidential Inaugural Address (1994)**
    - **Why It's Iconic:** Mandela's speech celebrated unity in South Africa's first multiracial democratic election and symbolized reconciliation after decades of apartheid.
    - **Key Lesson:** Speak of unity and forgiveness. A speech can heal wounds and chart a path toward collective progress.

6. **Barack Obama: "Yes We Can" Victory Speech (2008)**
    - **Why It's Iconic:** Obama's speech celebrated a historic moment, blending personal anecdotes, a hopeful vision, and inclusive language.
    - **Key Lesson:** Make your audience feel included. Speak in a way that empowers individuals to see themselves as part of the solution.

7. **Theodore Roosevelt: The Man in the Arena (1910)**
   - **Why It's Iconic:** Delivered in Paris, this speech emphasized the value of striving, failing, and trying again over sitting on the sidelines.
   - **Key Lesson:** Personalize inspiration. Use metaphors and stories to connect with your audience's challenges.

8. **Malala Yousafzai: United Nations Youth Assembly (2013)**
   - **Why It's Iconic:** Speaking after surviving a Taliban assassination attempt, Malala passionately advocated for girls' education worldwide.
   - **Key Lesson:** Speak from personal experience. Authenticity and conviction make your message unforgettable.

9. **Ronald Reagan: Speech at the Berlin Wall (1987)**
   - **Why It's Iconic:** Reagan's *"Mr. Gorbachev, tear down this wall!"* rallied for freedom and the eventual fall of the Berlin Wall.
   - **Key Lesson:** Use a defining phrase to drive home your message and make it memorable.

10. **Mahatma Gandhi: Quit India Speech (1942)**
    - **Why It's Iconic:** Gandhi called for non-violent resistance and independence from British rule, inspiring a movement that changed history.

- **Key Lesson:** Blend conviction with calmness. Persuasion doesn't always require loud words - sometimes, steady resolve is more powerful.

11. **Queen Elizabeth I: Speech to the Troops at Tilbury (1588)**
    - **Why It's Iconic:** Facing the threat of the Spanish Armada, Elizabeth rallied her troops with her famous line, *"I have the body of a weak and feeble woman; but I have the heart and stomach of a king."*
    - **Key Lesson:** Use your presence and passion to instill confidence in your audience.

Earlier in this book I did mention Marshall Ganz's that he taught me about the "Public Narrative" framework. It is a powerful storytelling method that combines personal connection, collective identity, and urgent action. Ganz teaches that a great story integrates three components:

1. **A Story of Self:** This is about who you are and why you care. It's your journey, the experiences, values, and choices that have shaped you and brought you to this moment.

    - **Purpose:** The Story of Self creates an emotional connection with your audience, building credibility and trust.
    - **Key Question:** What has called you to act?
    - **Example:** A speaker advocating for climate action might share a childhood story of growing up near a

forest that was destroyed by deforestation, shaping their commitment to the environment.

2. **A Story of Us:** This is about shared values and collective identity. It connects your personal story to the experiences and values of your audience, showing how "we" are in this together.

    - **Purpose:** The Story of Us builds community and solidarity.
    - **Key Question:** What are our shared values, challenges, and hopes?
    - **Example:** The same speaker might then highlight how their audience also values clean air, safe water, and a livable planet, fostering a sense of unity and shared purpose.

3. **A Story of Now:** This is about urgency and action. It answers the question, why does this matter now, and what can we do about it? It turns the emotional and communal connection into a call to action.

    - **Purpose:** The Story of Now motivates immediate action by highlighting the stakes and providing a clear path forward.
    - **Key Question:** What choice do we face, and what action must we take together?
    - **Example:** The speaker might conclude by explaining how the audience can act to make a

difference, such as joining a campaign, advocating for legislation, or supporting sustainable practices.

How It All Comes Together

When woven seamlessly, these three stories create a narrative arc that moves people emotionally, builds trust, and inspires action.

Personally, many of the pictures and images I use in my presentations are from my own life, spanning from early childhood to the present. It's powerful to say you felt like an outsider, but it's even more impactful to show it, perhaps a picture of you in a crowd where you're the only Arab or the office door that was slammed in your face.

On the flip side, an image of the office building where you later received an award creates a vivid, emotional contrast. I always include a picture of my family as well; it instantly establishes a bond of trust and connection with the audience.

I think as a motivational speaker, it is your duty to take your audience on a transformative journey, guiding them to a place they may not have reached on their own. That is the essence of leadership.

As an example, I work on software designed to filter out low-quality meetings. When I talk about this topic, I show a picture of myself lying on the floor while my kids are playing "doctors" on me. Then I share a powerful story: just a week before that photo was taken, I had been picked up by an ambulance after suffering a severe anxiety attack caused by burnout, too many meetings at work.

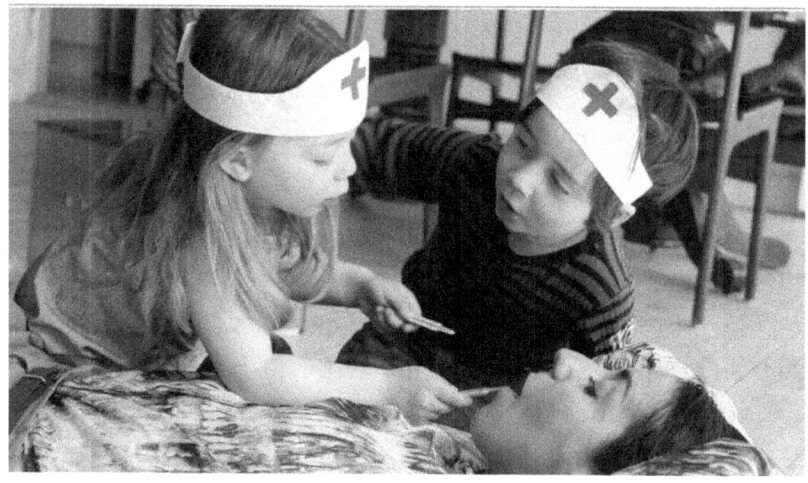

This story immediately grabs attention, sparks a serious conversation, and creates a genuine connection. It shows the *why* behind my work and helps people relate to the importance of solving this problem.

A great speaker motivates, inspires, provokes thought, moves hearts, and provides clarity. We don't just deliver words; we ignite action and leave our audience better equipped to face challenges and seize opportunities.

Audiences today expect more than generic speeches. They want personalized, relevant content that addresses their needs. We as speakers will need to embrace data and insights to craft tailored messages that engage and inspire, showcasing adaptability as a core skill for success.

When structuring your talk, aim for what I call the 30/70 split: 30% personal stories and 70% data, stats, or the main topic. Personal stories build connection, while data delivers credibility and impact.

Remember, 50% of the reason people listen to you is because they trust and like you. Sharing relatable stories allows the audience to see who you are, while the facts you present keep them engaged and informed. It's about balance, earning trust first, then delivering value.

Trust isn't just an ingredient in public speaking, it's the foundation. Without it, your message fades into noise. With it, you can move minds and inspire action.

True trust also demands credibility, earned through knowledge, preparation, and transparency. Audiences can spot a fraud; they don't just hear your words; they feel your intention. Overpromising or simplifying tough realities might win applause in the moment but erodes trust in the long run.

The most impactful speakers don't just motivate; they guide. They combine hard truths with hopeful possibilities. They balance data with humanity, leaving audiences not just inspired but equipped for action. Trust doesn't come from talking *at* people, it comes from speaking *with* them, creating a shared space where real change begins.

In public speaking, trust isn't given, it's earned. And when you earn it, you don't just hold an audience's attention, you hold their belief. Great speeches combine clarity, emotion, and connection. Sheryl Sandberg's TED Talk on gender equality blends personal stories with compelling data, striking a balance between relatability and authority. This mix of ethos (credibility), pathos (emotion), and logos (logic) makes her message persuasive and inspiring.

Though, one problem with some speakers is that they make tough problems sound too simple. They use catchy slogans or inspirational quotes that might sound great but don't offer real, practical advice. This can make people believe that just feeling motivated is enough to solve their challenges, when hard work and smart planning are often needed.

As journalist Edward R. Murrow puts it, *"Our greatest obligation is not to confuse slogans with solutions."*

There are many other frameworks you can be inspired by often used to guide speakers in storytelling and presentations:

1. **A Flower**
    - Start with a clear, strong central idea (the stem) and let it unfold into vibrant, engaging details (the petals).

2. **A FISH** (First In, Still Here)
    - Start strong, maintain audience attention throughout, and finish with impact—leaving the message lingering in their minds.

3. **A Mountain**
    - Build anticipation as you ascend (introduce conflict or ideas), reach a peak (the climax), and smoothly descend with resolution.

4. **A Journey/Map**
    - Take the audience on a journey with a beginning (where we are), a middle (challenges/insights), and an end (the destination or takeaway).

5. **A Sandwich**
   - Start and end with strong, memorable points (the bread), while the core content (the filling) is rich and satisfying.

6. **A Ripple**
   - Start with a small, focused idea and let it expand outward, touching broader themes as the story grows.

7. **The Rule of Three**
   - Break your story into three key parts (setup, conflict, resolution)—this resonates naturally with audiences and is easy to follow.

8. **The Puzzle**
   - Begin with intrigue (a missing piece), gradually reveal key parts, and complete the picture with the final takeaway.

9. **A Campfire Story**
   - Engage the audience intimately, as though you're telling a vivid, personal tale around a fire—be conversational, evocative, and relatable.

10. **The Movie Trailer**
    - Think of your story like a movie trailer if you want to **build momentum and excitement**—perfect for when you're promoting a show, selling tickets, or launching an event. Start with a

powerful hook to grab attention, tease the highlights (the "wow" moments), and build anticipation without giving everything away. Leave the audience with a clear call to action and a feeling of "I can't miss this!" This approach turns your presentation into an experience that excites and motivates people to show up for your show.

My personal favorite is The Hero's Journey Structure:

1. **The Ordinary World**

    Set the Scene: Start by describing a relatable situation your audience understands or has experienced. *Example*: "A few years ago, I was just like many of you, stuck in a job I didn't love, going through the motions every day." I strongly recommend using a powerful image, a brief audio clip, or another engaging element to support your point. Tap into your audience's emotions and bring your message to life.

2. **The Call to Adventure**

    Introduce the Challenge: Present the problem, opportunity, or turning point that changed everything. *Example*: "Then I got laid off. It felt like my world collapsed, but it was the push I needed to start my own business."

3. **Refusal of the Call**

    Show Vulnerability: Talk about the doubts, fears, or resistance you faced initially. This makes you relatable and human. *Example*: "At first, I didn't believe I could do it. Who was I to start a company? I almost gave up before I even started."

4. **Meeting the Mentor**

   Share the Guidance: Mention a mentor, book, resource, or insight that gave you the tools or confidence to move forward. *Example*: "A mentor told me, 'You don't need to know everything, just start.' That advice changed my mindset."

5. **Crossing the Threshold**

   Take the Leap: Describe how you stepped out of your comfort zone and acted. *Example*: "I took the little savings I had and launched my first product. I was terrified but also excited."

6. **Tests, Allies, and Enemies**

   Share Challenges and Wins: Talk about obstacles you faced, the people who helped you, and how you overcame adversity. *Example*: "There were rejections, failures, and moments when I thought I'd lose everything, but my team and mentors kept me going."

7. **The Ordeal**

   The Big Moment: Highlight the major struggle or turning point, your make-or-break moment. *Example*: "I had one last chance to pitch to a big client. I put everything into that meeting, and it paid off."

8. **The Reward**

Share the Win: Describe what you achieved - success, insight, or growth - and why it matters. *Example*: "That deal didn't just save my business; it taught me that perseverance beats fear every time."

9. **The Road Back**

    Bring It Home: Reflect on what you learned and how it can apply to others. *Example*: "Looking back, I realize the hardest part was starting. Everything else came with time."

10. **The Resurrection**

    Your Transformation: Show how the experience changed you or your outlook. *Example*: "I'm no longer afraid of failing. I'm more afraid of not trying."

11. **Return with the Elixir**

    The Lesson for the Audience: End with a takeaway - what the audience can learn, apply, or feel inspired by. *Example*: "If there's one thing, I hope you take away, it's this: Your greatest challenge might just be your biggest opportunity."

Here's a slide with my childhood photo, a snapshot of how my life unfolded, all on one slide. Simple, powerful, and relatable.

Homeless at the age of 13.

7th-grade school dropout.

"A homeless child can grow up to one day lead a multi-billion-dollar tech startup."

Remembering what Steve Jobs said in 1994: "The most powerful person in the world is the storyteller. The storyteller sets the vision, values, and agenda of an entire generation that is to come".

Types of Stories in Public Speaking

- **Personal Stories**: Sharing personal experiences builds authenticity and emotional connection. A childhood memory or life lesson can reveal values and motivations that resonate deeply with listeners. It's hard to tell your own story without involving others. Always respect privacy or seek consent when sharing someone else's story.
- **Others' Stories**: Highlighting someone's resilience or success, like a colleague's journey from failure to triumph, illustrates universal themes of perseverance and achievement.
- **Brand and Organization Stories**: Examples, like Ludwick Marishane's invention of DryBath,

showcase creative solutions to broader challenges while educating and inspiring audiences.

The Power of Storytelling in Presentations

A well-told story, structured with a clear beginning, middle, and end, draws listeners in, builds emotional connection, and makes messages memorable.

Key Storytelling Strategies

1. **Simplicity**: Keep narratives focused on one main idea; avoid unnecessary details.
2. **Engagement**: Start with a hook, like a question or surprising fact, to grab attention early.
3. **Emotional Connection**: Share relatable challenges and triumphs to evoke emotion.
4. **Audience Awareness**: Tailor stories to fit your audience's interests and experiences for maximum impact.

What Makes a Presentation Successful?

The best executive presentations share key ingredients: meticulous preparation, audience awareness, and seamless use of visuals to enhance the message. By studying these success stories, you can adopt proven strategies, like storytelling, emotional appeal, and tailored delivery, to elevate your public speaking and leave a lasting impact.

Your Next Step

As you step onto the path of becoming a truly memorable speaker, remember that the journey is as personal as it is practical. Every great speaker starts with small steps, and every meaningful change begins with a clear intention. Becoming the speaker, you dream of isn't about instant perfection, but about embracing growth and showing up authentically, time and time again. Being a great speaker isn't about perfection! Show more of yourself. Great speakers hold a remarkable advantage because they:

- master their subject,
- stay calm under pressure, and
- have the power to influence.

When learned, public speaking becomes a true game-changer.

Stand Tall and Own Your Space

Confidence begins before you speak, through your posture, presence, and energy. Avoid clinging to the podium. I often notice speakers who seem intimidated by the room, standing so close to their slides, that it's almost as if they want to hug them. They keep as far away from the audience as possible, avoiding eye contact and missing the chance to truly connect.

Use the stage fully and naturally, maintaining eye contact, pausing, smiling, and creating moments of connection. People are drawn to speakers who project calm, assured energy. Think of your movement on stage as "blocking" in theater. Move to a specific spot for each part of your story or key point. For example:

- Start your opening at center stage.
- Walk left to share a challenge or conflict.
- Move right to deliver your solution or closing. Intentional movement keeps your audience visually engaged and reinforces your message.

When you speak, let your hands bring emphasis and clarity to your words. Purposeful gestures are powerful allies in communication. Let them complement, not overwhelm, your message, and allow your hands to fall naturally by your side when not in use.

Speak at a pace that allows your words to breathe. Pauses aren't moments to fill; they're moments to let your ideas land and resonate. Stay present on stage, unafraid to take up space, pausing purposefully to allow your message to settle.

Move around naturally (without pacing, of course). Dare to make eye contact, pause, smile, and truly *be* in the moment. When you embrace the stage and engage with your audience, you create a connection that transforms a presentation into an experience.

Open with Sincerity

Your first impression matters. Within the first 7 seconds of opening your mouth, people decide whether they'll listen to you or mentally check out, pick up their iPhones, and start scrolling. Make those first moments count. Grab their attention immediately and hold it. I have a friend who starts her talk by unexpectedly singing, and it works every time.

Start with intention. Establish an immediate connection with your audience by expressing gratitude and sharing why this matters to you. If you aren't genuinely invested in your message, your audience won't be either. Speak with passion, tell your story, and invite listeners to join you in your purpose. Ask a question... and wait. Ask a thought-provoking or unexpected question early on and pause to let it sink in. Don't answer it immediately. This motivates your audience to engage with your message because their brains start working to find the answer.

Most people don't realize this: your audience isn't rooting for you to fail. They're silently cheering you on. Why? Watching someone struggle is uncomfortable for everyone. Your success puts them at ease and makes their time feel well spent.

Avoid Monotony, Stay Fresh

Even the most talented performers can fall into the trap of repetition. Stig Rossen (a musician) became so bored from performing the same role in *Les Misérables* night after night that he fell asleep on stage mid-performance. Don't let this happen to you. Change up your routine, stay present, and treat every speech as an opportunity to connect with your audience.

Consider using technology like live polls, quizzes, and questionnaires boosts real-time audience interaction, creating a dynamic and engaging presentation that encourages participation and enhances communication.

A few years ago, I was so focused on getting things done that I could handle 3-6 speaking gigs in a single day. My driver waited for me, taking me from place to place while I ate, slept, and even changed clothes in bathrooms along the way. My PA had everything prepped - AV, tech - you name it. I was literally running from one venue to the next. But here's what I missed: who I was speaking to. I failed to stop, pause, and truly understand my audience.

Knowing your audience is the foundation of impactful public speaking. Understanding their demographics, like age, background, values, and experiences, lets you tailor your message to connect, not just speak. Without that connection, even the most polished speech can fall flat. Your words need to resonate with *their* world, or you risk being just another voice they'll forget. Public speaking isn't about rushing through the day from venue to venue, it's about making each moment count for the people listening.

Be Memorable

Your audience will forget statistics and facts, but they will remember stories, images, and feelings. Bring something unique, a personal story, humor, visuals, or a bold opinion. People don't remember flawless speakers; they remember real ones. Wear Something Memorable! It doesn't have to be loud or flashy, just unique to *you*. A bright scarf, funky socks, a pin with a story, or even a pair of sneakers with a colorful suit. This not only helps people remember you but also gives you a fun talking point to break the ice.

Energy is Everything

Your energy, enthusiasm, and authenticity are your superpowers. Balance is key, too much energy without focus can overwhelm, while too little energy can lose room. Bring warmth, positivity, and calm confidence to the stage. If you are nervous, imagine you're speaking to one person, not a crowd. Pick a friendly face, maintain eye contact with them for a thought or sentence, and then shift naturally to someone else. It creates intimacy and energy in a room of hundreds and makes everyone feel seen.

Slides

Every slide should stand on its own, able to close your talk if time runs short. Don't click through a dozen slides frantically to reach your final point. Simplify. Better yet, skip the slides entirely and bring a whiteboard. A live, interactive session keeps your audience engaged and allows you to adapt in real time. If you use slides, tools like Beautiful.AI, Tome, Canva, and Gamma can help you create visuals that enhance, not distract.

Use Props, but Use Them Well

Bring a physical object that relates to your story or message, a broken clock, a handwritten letter, an old toy. Show it at just the right moment to create an emotional connection. A simple, unexpected prop can leave a lasting impression.

The human brain is wired to remember surprises and the unexpected like props. When something breaks a pattern or defies expectations, it grabs attention and sticks. Surprise triggers dopamine, which helps the brain pay attention and remember your message. Use it wisely to make your ideas unforgettable.

Speak to the Back Row

When you talk, imagine your words landing in the lap of the person sitting farthest from you. This naturally lifts your voice, slows you down, and improves your projection. It also helps you avoid sounding rushed or timid. Some speakers can be loud, but being loud doesn't always mean being effective. Volume alone can grab attention, but it's presence, tone, and clarity that keep people engaged.

Plan Your Exit, Literally

Don't just finish your speech and freeze. Plan your physical exit: step off the stage confidently, wave, or even walk into the crowd. Your last impression is just as important as your first, so leave with the same energy you brought. End with purpose, leaving your audience inspired, resolved, or hopeful. Your closing is your legacy, let it linger long after the applause fades. Finish while they're still engaged, still wanting more, and your message will echo in their minds.

Practical Steps to Keep Growing

1. **Your blurb?** Boil your talk down to a single sentence. If someone asked, "What's your speech about?" you should be able to answer in one clear line.
2. **Practice Relentlessly**: Growth requires consistent effort. Speak often, seek feedback, and refine your skills daily.
3. **Find Opportunities**: Don't wait for an audience, go out and find them. Look for local gatherings, online groups, or workshops.
4. **Make Yourself Accessible**: Add a booking link to your homepage, be on TikTok, YouTube etc. and set up a

scheduler on LinkedIn, and be proactive about creating opportunities.
5. There are countless groups on Facebook and LinkedIn actively looking for speakers for events. Join a few of them to explore opportunities and see what's out there, you might be surprised at how many stages are waiting for someone like you.
6. **Never Stop Learning**: Stay curious, update your content, and invest in your development. Excellence is a continuous journey.

Stories to be inspired from:

1. **The Terrified Beginner Who Forgot Her Script**

    The Situation: Emma, a first-time speaker at a local event, spent weeks perfecting her slides and memorizing her script. But as she stepped onto the stage, her mind went blank. Her slides didn't help. She clung to the podium, her voice faltering, as the audience quietly checked their phones. The more she noticed them tuning out, the more her words tumbled over each other. Her palms grew sweaty, her confidence crumbled, and she wished she could disappear from the stage.

    The Shift: Midway, she remembered something her mentor once told her: "People want you, not your script." Taking a deep breath, Emma let go of the podium, looked up, smiled, and spoke with sincerity.

    She shared a brief but moving story: her parents went bankrupt when she was a child, and ever since, she's been driven by a passion to teach financial literacy. In that moment, she built trust and connection with her audience.

The Outcome: The room came back to life. People leaned in, and one audience member said afterward, "I didn't care about your slides, I cared about *you*."

Lesson: A strong opening and authenticity trump a perfect script. Speak with intention, connect, and let your story shine. Before you say a single word let the silence stretch for 3-5 seconds. It feels counterintuitive, but it captures attention immediately. People stop, notice, and think, *"Something's happening."* Silence creates power and presence.

2. The Slide Hugger Who Found the Stage

The Situation: Mark had a habit of standing awkwardly close to his slides, as though they were his safety net. He avoided eye contact, barely moved, and clicked nervously through his deck. After his talk, someone joked, "Great slides, wish you'd been part of the presentation."

The Shift: Determined to improve, Mark practiced moving around naturally and ditching his slides when necessary. At his next talk, he swapped his deck for a whiteboard. He engaged the audience by asking questions, drawing visuals in real-time, and sharing stories.

The Outcome: People stayed glued to his every word. One attendee said, "It felt like a conversation, not a lecture."

Lesson: Dare to use the stage. Move with confidence, interact with your audience, and make every moment an experience.

3. **The Passionate Speaker Who Talked Too Fast**

   The Situation: Sarah loved her topic so much that she spoke at lightning speed. She crammed 50 ideas into 20 minutes, leaving her audience overwhelmed and exhausted. At the end, someone asked, "What was that middle part about again?"

   The Shift: After feedback, Sarah learned the power of the pause. She practiced speaking at a slower pace, emphasizing key points, and letting her ideas breathe. Instead of rushing, she paused intentionally, made eye contact, and smiled. She decided to end with a call to action: "When you leave this room, I challenge you to write down one goal and take one step toward it today."

   The Outcome: Her audience relaxed and absorbed her message. One listener said, "Your pauses and call to action made me reflect, your words landed."

   Lesson: Let your words breathe. Pauses are not gaps; they are opportunities for impact.

4. **The Over-Rehearsed Pro Who Lost the Spark**

   The Situation: James had delivered the same talk dozens of times. He was flawless - but robotic. One day, during a big event, he noticed attendees yawning, and one even checked their watch. He realized he had become "too perfect" and boring.

The Shift: Inspired by the Stig Rossen story, James decided to shake things up. He added new stories, adjusted his tone, and allowed spontaneity into his delivery. He treated each talk as a fresh opportunity to connect with *this* audience. He did then start with a question to ignite curiosity in his audience, instead of overwhelming them with facts or expertise. He said: "What if I told you we could reverse aging? Let me explain."

The Outcome: His energy returned, and so did the audience's excitement. A participant told him, "It felt like you were talking *to us*, not just reciting a speech."

Lesson: Avoid becoming stale. Keep your content fresh, adapt to your audience, and stay present in the moment.

5. **The Reluctant Speaker Who Took a Leap**

    The Situation: Mia was terrified of speaking and avoided opportunities at all costs. One day, her manager asked her to present a project update. She spent the night before in panic, imagining everything going wrong.

    The Shift: Instead of focusing on herself, Mia thought about the value she could share. She practiced opening with a heartfelt story and made sure to look up and smile. She reminded herself, "They're here to learn something, not to judge me." And she closed with a personal revelation, and some actionable advice: "Here's how 5 minutes a day can change your life."

    The Outcome: Her talk wasn't perfect, but it was real. Her authenticity won the audience over. A colleague discreetly slipped a note into her hand, offering feedback that simply read: "I felt like you cared about what you were saying, that's what made it SO powerful."

Lesson: Confidence grows when you shift the focus from yourself to your message. Show up, share what matters, and trust that your audience is on your side.

Suggested Reading List for Speakers Who Want to Deeply Understand Public Speaking.

Classic Texts on Public Speaking

1. "The Art of Public Speaking" by Dale Carnegie. A timeless guide that tackles stage fright, content organization, and audience engagement. Carnegie's emphasis on preparation, practice, and inspiring emotion makes this a foundational resource.
2. "Public Speaking" by J. Albert Winans. A historical text offering deep insights into speech structure and audience connection, laying the groundwork for modern speaking techniques.
3. "Essentials of Effective Speaking" by Howard Mosher. Focuses on spontaneous delivery and effective use of gestures to improve speaker engagement.

Additional Influential Reads

4. "Talk Like TED" by Carmine Gallo. An analysis of TED Talks that highlights storytelling, emotional connection, and practical techniques for creating compelling presentations.
5. "Resonate: Present Visual Stories that Transform Audiences" by Nancy Duarte

Communication and Rhetoric

6. "Thank You for Arguing" by Jay Heinrichs. A modern guide to the art of persuasion, blending humor, historical examples, and rhetorical strategies for engaging audiences effectively.
7. "The Rhetoric of Fiction" by Wayne C. Booth. Explores narrative techniques that help speakers craft compelling and persuasive presentations.
8. "Techniques of Persuasion: The Art of Influence." A comprehensive resource on rhetorical tools and strategies that enhance persuasive communication.

The Final Word

Congratulations on making it to the end of this guide. If you take only one thing away, let it be this: Speaking is an art, a craft, and a commitment. Whether you're just starting or are a seasoned speaker, these final reminders will help you connect, captivate, and leave a lasting impression.

Don't Be Afraid to Steal the Spotlight

Claim your space. Set the tone. Many speakers hold back, waiting for permission, but don't. Take charge, and people will follow your lead.

Mastering being a speaker takes practice, but they form the backbone of powerful public speaking. By embodying presence, passion, and poise, you'll not only capture attention, but you'll also inspire, engage, and leave a lasting impression. And remember don't just share scars; share how you healed.

The number one thing people hate about public speakers. Being boring or inauthentic. So, whatever you do, don't be that person.

I was speaking in the Nordics this summer, and a woman spoke before me. She was brilliant, her content was excellent, but all people talked about afterward was how sad it was that she couldn't move her face (likely due to Botox).

When striving to look great, remember this: your facial expressions are a key part of how you connect with your audience. If your face can't move, neither can your emotions, and that's what people relate to most.

Studies show that when you're nervous about speaking, your body releases adrenaline, the same chemical released in life-threatening situations. This is why public speaking feels like a "fight or flight." The brain doesn't distinguish between a tiger chasing you and an audience staring at you. Practice mastering your nerves. When I practiced for my TEDx talk, I learned the power of sitting in silence, taking off my shoes, grounding myself, and listening to meditation music. I sometimes still wear high heels on stage, but what you don't see is what happens right before I step into the spotlight. I sit quietly, plant my feet firmly on the ground, and breathe deeply. I boost my mindset, center my energy, and prepare myself. So, when I walk on stage, I'm not just walking, I'm ready. Ready to connect, deliver, and own the moment.

Ok, before I let you go, I have a small request: if you found this book helpful, I hope you'll share it and recommend it. Your support helps this book, and these ideas, reach more people who need them. Thank you for reading, and here's to making your next talk unforgettable!

Good Luck! Now go out there and be the speaker they never forget.

Disclaimer: The content in this book is a synthesis of publicly available data, personal observations from decades of speaking experience, and insights from industry experts. Every effort has been made to ensure originality and avoid any unintentional use of proprietary information.

www.ingramcontent.com/pod-product-compliance
Lightning Source LLC
Chambersburg PA
CBHW071037240526
45469CB00006BD/2239